Con[illegible]ng

BE SEEN BE HEARD BE YOU!

So That Your Ideal Client Wants To Do Business With You

CHERYL CHAPMAN

AND THE CONFIDENT SPEAKERS

Orders: Please contact support@cheryl-chapman.com.
You can also order via the email address
support@cheryl-chapman.com

ISBN: 978-0-9934587-4-3

First published 2021. Updated 2022, 2023 & 2024

Confidently Come Speaking

BE SEEN
BE HEARD
BE YOU!

So That Your Ideal Client Wants To Do Business With You

CHERYL CHAPMAN

AND THE CONFIDENT SPEAKERS

Breakfree Forever Publishing

Foreword by Secret Millionaire Dr. Dawn Gibbins MBE

As founder and leader of a global company for 30 years, I delivered speeches in many countries on transformational leadership and business success.

I was so proud to promote my team and our products. After selling my company for millions of pounds, I embarked on a new journey in life to find my true self (the real authentic me), and then teach people how to find their true inner nature.

When it came to speaking and promoting myself - wow! This was so different from doing what I did in the corporate world! There, I told everyone:

'Self-promotion is not a sin'

And yet, when it came to promoting myself, I had shrivelled and lost my confidence.

I heard about the *Confidently Come Speaking* opportunity with Cheryl Chapman and I knew I would benefit from her guidance, as we had worked together before.

Cheryl helped me find clarity and confidence. She challenged me on every aspect of my offerings, and made suggestions to make the presentation even better. Most of all, Cheryl believed in me and mentored me to discover the message I needed to help transform people's lives. In all my experience of public speaker trainers, Cheryl Chapman is the best I have ever experienced.

Cheryl trains from her heart, and her passion for your success shines through in all her training.

I believe Cheryl Chapman is one of the greatest speaker trainers in the world.

I am so proud now to have a professional recording of my presentation 'Dare to be Different' and the interview with Cheryl, where I share my products and services to help others.

I am excited to announce that I am a published author, award-winning speaker and a mid-Life woman who is living on purpose and sharing my truth.

Dr. Dawn Gibbins MBE

Contents

Preface

Wise words have been shared in communities for centuries by the oracles, the chiefs, and the WHYs ones, the ones that know their WHY; they have a purpose and share their passion with other members of the community. Usually, the WHYs ones are the older members, the ones that have lived a full and rich life, the ones with the scars to prove they have been around the block a few times. These are the ones who help others, the ones you go to for help, the 'everyday influencers', the ones who will tell you the truth, based on their own experiences. If you want to share your wisdom, there are a few things you might like to know from those who have gone before you. This book will explore the following points of wisdom from confident speakers, and the questions they would raise or answer if you wanted them to help you to share your wisdom too:

Wisdom 1 - Why Are You Invisible To The People You Can Serve?

In order for people to know you're alive, you need to be visible. They need to SEE you! I know you might be thinking: *No Shit Sherlock*! Why then, are there so many people hiding?

Wisdom 2 - Do People Buy People?

Yes and No!

It's possible to buy something from someone you don't know as long as you want it! Think about the smiling lady in the supermarket (who you've never met before), who offers you a taste of some cheese on a stick, that turns into a packet of cheese in your trolley! However, if it was your mum and you don't like cheese, it doesn't matter how close you are...no purchase!

What if you don't like the person?

It's highly unlikely, you'll do business with them, right?

Unless they are the only person with that solution, for example, selling water in a desert, being able to teach you a skill that is imperative or like the water seller, they have a monopoly in the market.

Why?

Because the reality is you don't really buy people, you buy the solution to a problem you want resolving.

Wisdom 3 - Why Is Trust Crucial In Relationships?

If you don't trust others, then the chance of a transaction is reduced, even if you do feel thirsty! I mean how can you trust that the water is safe to drink, if the person handing it to you looks dirty or smiles at you like an assassin, when they hand the bottle to you?

And the truth is, trust can be broken in seconds. Think about the last time someone you trusted, let you down. There is another question here, and that is do you TRUST yourself? Because the truth is, if you don't trust yourself, why should anyone else?

And why don't you trust yourself?

Wisdom 4 - Why Is It Easier to Share Your Passion?

Do you really know WHY you are here and WHY you are doing what you are doing right now? Is it your dream life or someone else's? When you know WHY you are on this planet (not just to eat, shit and die), when your life has meaning, and you become more passionate. This passion and enthusiasm for life means others will follow your energy.

It's like meeting someone for the first time and you don't know why, but you just want to hang around with them and be in their aura of positivity.

I have experienced the power of when you Find Your WHY first-hand and with *The Find Your WHY Foundation*, created by myself and Marion Bevington.

Whereas your WHY, is why you are where you are right now, what works for you, and what potentially holds you back. We love guiding others to overcome the blocks and barriers that stop them being even more *frickin'* awesome and living the life they were born to have.

Wisdom 5 - How Far Ahead of Someone Do You Need To Be to Help Them?

Be confident to know you only need to be one step ahead to help someone! Many people try to become so educated in their specialised area, that they have no time to serve those who could already benefit from what they know.

As a coach, consultant, therapist and wise one, you will no doubt have experienced some pain in the area that you now help others to get away from, or even avoid. Right now, they need your support, not in a year's time when you might feel more qualified - you already know more than enough.

Wisdom 6 - Does Striving for Perfection Kill Dreams?

It certainly can, waiting until you are perfect is the perfect way of wasting your life. Thinking about what you want to do, will never achieve anything. Achievement is the result of action, aka, move your ass!

Wisdom 7 - Why Do People Procrastinate?

There can be many reasons and yet when you dive deeper, it appears to link back to one thing...

The fear of judgement. The thought of being judged can lead to procrastination. If you don't complete something, no-one can judge it, right?

And if you have ever caught yourself distracted from the task at hand (think numerous cups of tea/ coffee, biscuits, watching shit TV programs, Facebook, gossiping with friends or even excessive cleaning), when you have an important task to do, then you too have been putting things off.

Wisdom 8 - Why Don't I Feel Like I'm Good Enough?!

Here the feeling of not feeling good enough can be because of many reasons; comparison, judgement or because someone once treated you as if you were worthless.

In the words of one of my mentors, Marisa Peer:

You are enough, you always have been, and you always will be. The great news is, that the experiences you have had in the past, don't have to dictate your future.

And now a question for you - are ready to share your wisdom? You are? Great 🧜‍♀️...

Let's go!

With love,
Cheryl x

However, before we begin, there is something you may want to know about me...

I'd like you to remember a time when you felt judged.

Not a nice thought I know, but please bear with me.

It's November 5th, 2019, the night in the UK that we celebrate by burning an effigy of a man called Guy Fawkes, who was part of a conspiracy group that failed to blow up the Houses of Parliament. I'm sitting in my home office in Huddersfield, West Yorkshire in the UK. It's a converted cow barn in the middle of a field and my office is on the lower ground floor, overlooking an acre of land, which in the daytime is beautiful and at night is pitch black, and the deathly silence is only interrupted with the occasional hoot of an owl. Except tonight, the air is filled with the cracking and whizzing of fireworks in the background, as a reminder of the explosion that never happened back in 1605.

Thinking about that time in history, there was a lot of judging going on. The conspirators were judging the monarchy and of course when they were betrayed, they were all judged ultimately with the consequence of prison or death!

Looking through my emails, suddenly there's like a little ping and the notification in the top right of my computer, catches my eye. TED.com...oh, how exciting this must be about the final plans for the forthcoming TEDxWomen event I'm organising. Let's see what this is all about. Little did I know what I was about to read.

CHAPTER 1

Betrayal To Bold

Email from TED.com

> *Hi Cheryl,*
> *I hope this finds you well!*
>
> *We're reaching out as it has come to our attention that you are offering speaker coaching services for a fee to prospective TEDxAinleyTopWomen speakers in exchange for a spot onstage, which is outside of our guidelines and against the spirit of the TEDx platform.*
>
> *Please discontinue any paid speaker coaching services*
>
> *immediately and refund any individuals who have already paid you for this service.*
>
> *We'd be grateful if you could confirm your understanding around this, as well as confirmation that all speakers have been refunded, as soon as possible.*
>
> *Thank you and we look forward to your response by* **Thursday 7 November.**

It's interesting how, looking back, they were very polite in their request and actually only putting boundaries in place, right? However, at the time, it was like I was really being told off and isn't it strange how the words always seem loud? It's always serious!

Do you ever read emails and feel like you're being judged?

The truth is, this wasn't about asking '*for a fee to prospective* TEDxAinley Top Women speakers *in ex-change for a spot onstage*,' it was about standards. It was about my reputation because speaker training is how I earn a living. Because I'm an international multi-award-winning speaker/speaker trainer, darling! You can just hear the ego right 😳.

Seriously, I have been coaching entrepreneurs, employees and enlightened souls in the advice sharing world, for nearly a decade and I have been sharing my own message (helping others to find their WHY) through presentations in person and online. So, I know when I hear a great presentation - and I know when I hear one that isn't.

The trouble is most of the submissions were good and, with some direction, they could be great, yet they were also not in keeping with the spirit of TED which is to 'spread great ideas.'

Most of the talks submitted to me are about the speaker's personal journey or about their products and services and, whilst these are empowering and life changing experiences, on a TED stage these are a no-no. What would you do if you had an ability to help someone else make a change with your skills and expertise?

I'm sure, like me, you'd want to help, right? And the reality is, TED need to approve each and every talk before they load it onto their platform and, if it's not on the TED YouTube platform, well, it doesn't exist. Why? Because only TED have the copies of the presentations. Have you ever had a time when you wanted to justify what you were doing?

I wanted to go back to TED and say:

> *"Look I'm not making any profit from this – I'm offering my world class speaker coaching at a fraction of the cost my regular clients pay me and I won't be making any profit, because it's already cost me nearly 10 thousand pounds to put on this event, including £1,200 for the TEDx Ainley Top Women letters; a 12-foot glitter red shoe, to go with the BOLD theme at £700 to hire; £500 for more props, a red circle for the floor, hiring a venue, paying for promotional activity, hiring a professional videographer that can adhere*

to the very specific guidelines, sound, staging, food, and I've spent the last 6 months watching hundreds of TED videos and reading up on how to create a TED Talk. Now I'm expected to give my professional services for free? Not to make a profit, as it will barely cover the costs - it's because I want to support the speakers to reach TED standards, my standards and so when their family and friends watch them now or in the future, they can be proud of what they created."

But I didn't say anything.

Why? Because the truth is, there is no point. TED have rules, of course they do. They have a brand to protect, and I've already had 6 months of learning to agree with these rules, to get the licence in the first place. But there is something else that is bigger than TED's guidelines and their perceived judgement of my behaviour - it's the feeling of BETRAYAL. The only way TED could know about this, is because one of the speakers must have told them. That's someone I know, someone I trust, someone

I'm trying to help. Have you ever had your trust broken? How did it feel for you? I felt like I'd been stabbed in the back, like I can't breathe. And a bigger feeling is that I didn't know which of the speakers it was, so now I felt like I had to watch my back. The questions in my pounding head were now leading to the tears falling from my face. Here's the dilemma, should I have carried on or given up?

What would you do in this type of situation?

Before I undertook my personal development journey, I'll be honest, I would have hit the alcohol and phoned anyone who would listen to me bitching and moaning about the situation all while pretending I didn't give a shit!

Well, the good news is that I've learned a few lessons in my 59 years around the sun (and in particular over the last 13 years), and one is that this kind behaviour doesn't serve anyone!

I decided to be honest with those involved, show my vulnerability, and share how upset I felt about the situation, whilst asking if the person responsible would please let me know why they had gone to TED instead of speaking to me first. The speaker came forward and, as is often the case, there was a reason why, which was nothing to do with trying to stab me in the back. There was no treason or indeed a plot against me to bring down my support. The truth is, it had been someone she had been paying to coach her that had notified TED maybe because they felt judged by my comments on how her talk could be improved?

Isn't it strange how it is possible to create such a story in your head based on a little information?

And yet, as a trained Advanced Rapid Transformational Therapist, I support both my personal development and speaker clients, to understand that they create the world they live in based on the pictures in their mind and the words, they say to themselves. So, when they have moments of self-doubt, not feeling good enough, worrying about what others may say or even feeling like an imposter, I help them. to make changes to move to a more positive movie script!

I do remind myself and other mentors, coaches, or trainers that you could be the world's number one doctor when it comes to appendix removal and yet if you needed to do the operation on yourself, it would be messy and painful, right? So yes, I did have a moment of negative thoughts, but the great news is I quickly remembered the only way to resolve a situation with someone is to talk to the person you have the issue with - no-one else can do anything about it.

With the conversation over, I was able to move ahead with the plans. You may have already picked up on this, but this was a speaking event which was mainly for women. This is not because I don't like men (I've been engaged 4 times and tied the knot twice; I quite like men – or is it the fruit cake?) Seriously, it was because throughout my career and the subsequent work with both male and female clients, men generally will take more chances, whilst many women wait to be perfect.

I often hear the words:

"Just one more course."

"I just need to get these ducks in a row and then I'll be ready."

I believe this is because of the fear of judgement. Think about it. If you think about being judged (what people will think/say), do you think about the old man dressed in red and white?

No, not Father Christmas. I mean the judge with the gavel in his hand, waiting to bring it down and take away your freedom by putting you in jail?

This isn't your fault, because it goes back to a time well, before your birth when we used to live in tribes. The fear of being thrown out of the tribe in years gone by would, of course, mean certain death. How could 1 person protect themselves against the sabre-toothed tiger, without the support of the tribe?

It's not your fault if you do fear judgement, it's in your DNA!

That said, would you agree that it is easy to blame others or situations, to give yourself an excuse to not move forward?

I have spent the last 5 years helping other women to 'STOP bitching and start pitching!' The reason for this is that there are less women on stage and around the boardroom tables across the world, and so my belief is that if you want it, you have to get off your ass and make it happen. That is why, even though I did feel misunderstood and judged by TED, I decided that the show must go on for all the speakers who had decided to be brave and stand up to speak out. After all, I'd encouraged them to overcome the fear of judgement and so it would have been very hypocritical to run for the hills myself.

That's when the coaching began, I created a new process to ensure all the speakers were able to deliver in a way that was professional and entertaining and after watching hundreds of TED videos, I worked out what I believed TED wanted in a presentation. I guided all of the speakers and shared this system, and I included the mindset support too. This meant they could create their revised presentations and send me a video. Then I did what I've been doing for nearly a decade for entrepreneurs, employers, and enlightened souls. I provided honest feedback so they could make their presentations even more impactful. The TED Speakers in training put in the hours to rehearse - it was a perfect collaboration.

On Friday 13th December 2019, TEDxAinleyTopWomen went ahead. 20 speakers (19 women and 1 man - told you I wasn't against men), shared their messages of hope and help and I can tell you, on the day, we had a 100 strong audience who stayed all day to support all the speakers, and gave amazing feedback to myself and the whole crew. It was magical!

However, there was still another challenge ahead...

Picture this. I'm back in my office on the 6th of January 2020 and my phone, which is sitting on my desk, appears to be having a party of its own, vibrating and buzzing every few minutes. Eventually, I give in and take a look at the screen where all the WhatsApp messages are lined up:

- Lisa's talk has been approved by TED and it's on their website.
- Caroline's talk has been approved by TED and it's on their website.
- Wendy's talk has been approved by TED and it's on their website.
- 3 approvals turned into 6 and then 9 and 12, 15, 16, 17 and in between all the "*congratulations*" and "*I just watched your presentation, it was great*" messages, there was one that stood out from the rest:

"*Cheryl, my presentation hasn't been approved yet and I don't know if I can cope with this rejection on top of everything that has happened to me in the last 12 months. Please can you update me on why my talk hasn't passed – Kath x*

You know what it's like. The one person who really needs a boost, the one you've been supporting, who has been making some positive steps towards creating a new life (maybe for you it's been a friend, relative, client or even you), the one that need some reassurance and then it's like they get kicked in the teeth.

That is what was happening here.

It didn't make sense. Kath was an authentic speaker who, despite working in a highly stressful environment, presented on the topic of resilience something she shared with her team on a daily basis. On a personal level, Kath had experienced a year where she had used every ounce of her training for herself.

This was her area of expertise.

And so, the questions began. In fact, there were 2 talks that TED requested more evidence on. I do have to be honest that one of these talks was based on the subject of the healing powers of minerals. I was fascinated by this and yet I thought it may be outside of one of the TED rules:

The TED and TEDx are platforms for showcasing and explaining genuine advances in science that are backed by research. Scientific claims by speakers should be based on data that has survived scrutiny by experts in the field.

This speaker, Alijca, was a little more pragmatic and said "*I can get you all the evidence together.*" And that's exactly what we did, working with TED to get this information together, so that they allowed these 2 TEDxAinleyTopWomen presentations (Which you can view on Youtube along with the other 18 speakers), onto the TED platform.

Interestingly, Kath and Alijca's talks had the most views from all of the talks straight away!

Here are the links to all of the talks (which at the time of typing have approximately 40,000 views). That's 40,000 lives potentially touched by these amazing humans. I am so glad that I was able to help them be brave so they could be seen, be heard be themselves and confidently share their knowledge.

TEDxAinleyTopWomen 2019

Kath Wynne-Jones

The 3 F's of Resilience

https://youtu.be/TvSI4hwFU98

Alijca Son

Why Minerals rock!

https://youtu.be/_iYzUwTdqiA

Lisa King

Unmasking The True You

https://youtu.be/Pm3BPQxWTo8

Caroline Emile

Transforming an adversity into an advantage

https://youtu.be/wrVgn6hBjuY

Helen Bartram

Confessions Of A Guilty Mum

https://youtu.be/dDnOxFmOJkI

Dena Roering

Playful Grownups Overcoming Adversity

https://youtu.be/6UeJcPtrzvs

Deenita Pattni

Innovate Yourself Out Of Mediocrity

https://youtu.be/bJj243UjKWY

Bilyana Georgieva

How Executives Can Stop Wasting Time

https://youtu.be/eHpuWRDM_L4

Suzy Miller

"Peace Delusion In The War Of Divorce"

https://youtu.be/fXCzlobVmpo

Leila Singh

(Voted the 2nd best Female TEDxWomen Talk of 2020 by TEDxUnicatt)

Are You Just Another Number In Your Organisation?

https://youtu.be/YO5PO_YK58E

Ruth Driscoll

Don't Let Fear Interfear

https://youtu.be/yn6Vqvm5dkU

Martin Sharp

The Power of "AND"

https://youtu.be/hmaj_nq28Ag

Lesley Downs

Putting the Magic back into Marriage

https://youtu.be/S9I4JwW0jCY

Sam Stray Wood

Hit The Ground

https://youtu.be/9s3U9bj6-FY

Carole Fossey

The Secret of living (and social media) is Giving

https://youtu.be/V-S5lGbc72c

Wendy Sneddon

How Domestic Violence Affects Pets

https://youtu.be/utFuDvuBS1A

Sylvia Milton

Let's Get Britain Listening

https://youtu.be/l01lI-FQyhw

Lisa Zevi

Are All Roads In Your Business Still Leading To You?

https://youtu.be/IwENj3oWXiQ

Jo Corbishley

The Power of 3 Words

https://youtu.be/iQTyi0iq4JY

Marion Bevington

Are You Running Away from Something or Running To Something?

https://youtu.be/SJ_TqdwuxnM

So, what next?

Can you remember growing up how there is always the next step? I mean you go out with someone and the questions start:

> *"When will you make your relationship official, then it's when are you going to get engaged? Followed by will there be wedding bells, pitter patter of tiny feet (yes, I'm getting a dog...or was that just me* ☺*)"*

And likewise, the questions began again,

> *"Will you be applying for the licence again Cheryl?"*

It is true, I had become as popular as Bozo the Clown, with friend requests from unknown contacts increasing each day, via social media. Sometimes, it's difficult to know what to do for the best, isn't it?

Of course, I wanted to support and help others to be seen and heard but at the same time I knew that TED's rules would eliminate many of my "enlightened" and entrepreneurial clients from the experience because, as shown with Alijca's talk, they were not fully open to what may be referred to as '*pseudo-science*'.

Also, as the organiser I wasn't allowed to speak at the event (except as the compere) and I wanted to share my thoughts and ideas too. However, sometimes it's better to focus on the bigger picture. Knowing the power of this worldwide brand, the decision was more about how I could help others to be seen and heard which led to the application for 2020, even though the presentations had to be with either no audience or a small one, due to the pandemic.

Do you believe in fate?

I certainly do and I believe the universe had other plans for me because my application was rejected.

Yet another judgment, you might be thinking?

What do you do in a situation like this?

I did feel judged again. The wig. The gavel. The verdict.

The sense of belonging to the TED tribe was over in one email.

And yet it gave me a sense of freedom too.

Gemma, my sister who looks a little bit like me with black hair and much younger, is sitting opposite me in the office.

"Well, at least you don't have to follow the rules Chez. In fact, why don't you do your own event?"

"Call it CHEDx."

"Oh yeah Gem, that would go down well. You're the lawyer in the family, are you trying to get me into court?"

"Chez, like you said there are so many people that TED won't even allow on their platform and yet we know they still have a great message to share. Look at all the WHYs women and WHYs men that you have in your *Find Your WHY* Foundation. How many of them could be seen by others if you created a different type of offer?

"Gem, it sounds like a plan but who the hell am I compared to the machine that is TED?"

"Chez, think about what you did so that people could get to know you. In 2011, when you attended the event to see Bob Proctor in London, you were an employee, binge drinker, miserable, hated your life and after going on a personal journey of discovery with all its highs and lows, you found your WHY, your purpose.

to see Bob Proctor in London, you were an employee, binge drinker, miserable, hated your life and after going on a personal journey of discovery with all its highs and lows, you found your WHY, your purpose. Which is to guide other women to stop *asking why me*? and have the clarity and confidence to say *why not me*!

You've helped thousands of entrepreneurs, employees, employers and enlightened souls to share their messages, you helped Andy Harrington to build a multi-million pound business by developing the coaching side of his offer at the Professional Speakers Academy. You have also coached your mentees so they could stand on stages across the world. You've travelled around the world presenting to small, medium, and large audiences. You wrote an award winning book. You've been interviewed in countries where you can't even speak the language, and of course you've done pre-recorded and live videos on both social media and your website. So hmmm, let me see. You might not be an international celebrity but more of an 'Everyday Influencer'. Someone who helps everyday people help other everyday people. And, for what it's worth, that's more valuable to the masses than any organisation that is trying to control others with rules and regulations!"

'Queens of Life' Event in Poland with 2,500 people

Speaking in Singapore to 500 students

Being Interviewed on Slovenian TV

Power to Achieve Presenting to 500 Entrepreneurs

My 1st public speaking trainer award at The Professional Speakers Academy with founder Andy Harrington. I have held this title 3 times in total as well as *Female Speaker Presentation Skills* of the year.

I have to say that the 100s of awards my clients win is what I love best though

As well as personally mentoring thousands of entrepreneurs, employers, and enlightened souls to build their businesses; I also co-created The A.C.E. (*Academy Coaching Executive*) Accreditation Program with Deenita Pattni to train 50 coaches to mentor all around the world and support a multi-million-pound public speaking business.

Looking back at these words of wisdom from my younger sister, this was actually the beginning of The Confidently Come Speaking concept - a place where you can speak your truth with the confidence that as everyday influencers, you need to be seen, heard and be yourself. So that your ideal clients can get to know, like and trust you and learn about the solutions to their problems, through your products, services or ideas.

#confidentlycomespeaking

Of course, at the time, in 2020, we were in the middle of the COV-19 lockdown, and it seemed as though every man, woman and their dog had pivoted online, with videos, challenges and webinars, in an attempt to be seen by their existing and potential clients. Clearly, meeting in groups of any real size was out of the question and yet now was the time to be able to connect with other humans and to ignite new relationships. And so, it was time to adapt and change in a true entrepreneurial way - by thinking out of the box and looking at alternative options Gemma was right!

The way other people got to know about me (in the multi-speaker circle) initially, was that I was seen and heard. Thus

I needed to be memorable. Maybe it was the potty mouth (*occasionally I do drop an 'F-bomb'*), the innuendos in my talks, the humour, the self-deprecation or the fact that I bared my arse (metaphorically) about the drinking that I used to do to distract me from a life I didn't like. I believe from the comments, that it was because I was being myself (more about that later!)

In a world of 'pretending everything is OK', I guess I became comfortable with not being perfect and shared that (being honest here - it took some re-training!). I learned that being yourself is much easier than trying to be the person everyone else wanted you to be I wanted to help other coaches, consultants, entrepreneurs, employers, and enlightened souls to get their message out so others could find them and remember them too.

The TEDxAinleyTopWomen had been a starting point and now the Confidently Come Speaking events were another opportunity for this to happen on a less rigid basis.

At first, I was saying; I don't care what you want to speak about, and I don't care if you swear, you can tell your story or even speak about your products or service. All of which remain true, except of course if someone said they'd like to speak about how they murder people (I know it's the story telling mind again!)

However, I have a simple check, which is based on one of the mantras of my late cousin Lynsey (who died at just 27 with a condition called Cystic Fibrosis), which was to *Live Love and Laugh every day!*

So as long as you are sharing how you live your life, what you love, and what I know will put a smile on my face - well you've passed the first stage ☺

I believe that when you are able to share your truth in an Authentic way then you truly become the authority with your clients. Actually, I don't like the word authority.

In a recent poll, 80% of those asked what comes to mind when you hear this word, said something negative such as control, dictators, lack of freedom, or no choice. I prefer to think of it as you become an Everyday Influencer, which feels like there is more freedom.

Just 6 weeks later and the first presentations take place. 14 speakers all share their professional message, followed by them being interviewed by me so that they can show their personality. Finally, they are then included in this book, where you will be able to connect with them directly and watch their performances. To help guide them to prepare engaging, educational, and entertaining presentations, I created a program to help them be seen, heard and felt so that their ideal clients know, like and trust them.

I had the opportunity to share my thoughts by presenting my talk dressed as a clown. To help other everyday people understand how to overcome the fear of judgement (after all I'd had a lot of practice!).

In the presentation I actually get undressed on stage, but don't let that put you off!

If you'd like to watch the presentation, please click the link below:

"The Show Must Go On"

https://youtu.be/weGO8bHH9Os

The October event was sold out within days and so was the first date in 2021. I even had a piece written in my hometown's newspaper on the front cover of **The Fleetwood Weekly News** and The Lancashire Chronical. I was interviewed about the events, and I was part of 'The Girl that does Exhibition' at Fleetwood's Museum, it's a great feeling to be recognised and the excitement was growing for this new adventure. The Everyday Influencers were doing just that - helping and supporting others.

#Sensational

Fame at last!

CHAPTER 2

How To Be Confident

The first part of being confident is to be sensational.

You might be thinking, what do I mean by be SENSATIONAL?

Do I mean get yourself on the front of the newspapers for something inappropriate?

Of course, the answer is No!

By *sensational* I mean how can people (more specifically, your ideal client) get to experience you with as many senses as possible. In the main, this is how they can SEE you, HEAR you and FEEL you?

I know you might be thinking, hang on, I know I want to help my clients but "*feel*" me is taking it a bit far!

By *feel* I mean how can they get to know you better?

So that they get a good feeling about who you are, what you do and why you do what you do?

As a by-product of these 3 experiences, they also get to use the sense of taste (do you leave a good or bad taste in their mouth after an interaction with you?) or do they smell a rat when you are around them?

In reality it's how your potential clients get to experience the real you.

If you think about those that are the closest to you, they are more likely to know a lot more about you and vice-versa, therefore, your relationship is stronger. The problem is that most people think it takes years for people to really get to know you, and his was based on being able to gather together freely.

Now being more isolated than ever, how can you be with someone long enough to build this connection?

Firstly, it does not take years to become sensational. You may already be familiar with the belief that it *only takes 7 seconds to make a first impression and you only get one shot at a first impression!*

However, more recent studies from two Princeton psychologists Janine Willis and Alexander Todorov reveal it only takes a tenth of a second to form an impression of a stranger's face! Now add in voice, body language and your energy and that is going to give a stranger more of you to be impressed by, does that make sense?

A side note here and just for a bit of fun - you would know this is true if you ever watched the Naked Attraction series on channel 4 with Anna Richardson. If you haven't here's a brief 'overview'

> *`Naked Attraction', a dating show that begins where some dates may end, with all contestants naked.*
>
> *Singletons get up close and personal as they meet for the first time in their birthday suits, stripped of all clothes, make-up, and status symbols. Starting from their legs they reveal the torso (yep with all the bits on show!), head, and finally their voice. That's the SEE & HEAR covered the contestants get in touch (FEEL) with their primal instincts as they narrow down their potential match from a group of six nude hopefuls. This social experiment is inspired by evolutionary science, where it is believed that in the past people selected mates based only physical appearance.*

With this in mind, it is fair to say like 'traditional' dating, you really do have a better chance of getting to know someone with more time and interaction and with your clothes on! Which is good news for business connections.

The reason why it's imperative to be SEEN, HEARD and FELT can go hand in hand with a quote by Bob Burg, a networking and referral expert:

> ***All things being equal, people do business with, and refer business to people they know, like and trust.***
>
> - Bob Burg - *Endless Referrals*

I guess it won't come as a shock to you, if you have any products, services, or wisdom to share with others, that the fundamental principle behind others buying from you is that they need to know, like and trust you. This is the way to convert prospective clients into paying customers, whilst building a community of raving fans, who refer, buy from you and champion you to others.

The truth is people need to know you exist- otherwise you are invisible to them, making you the world's biggest secret to those who need you. I want to let you know that this is not a book on marketing, in the sense of here's what you can do with adverts on social media or how you can get yourself in the press (I do have some trusted marketing contacts that I can share with you to explore that further if you'd like).

This is a book on the power of connection and what "know, like and trust" all really mean?

KNOW

This step is all about visibility.

Before you can even think about supplying your products or services to someone, they first need to know you exist.

Seems straightforward, but for many entrepreneurs, getting visible is one of their primary challenges.

Are you the world's best kept secret?

Here's the thing, even if people know about you, unless you are already a friend, or being introduced by a friend, if they are about to do some business with you, most potential clients will google you - you've done this, right?

The question is do you pass the Google test?

I remember the first time I googled myself, I found another Cheryl Chapman from the USA talking about 'fluffing her breasts!'

However, whilst I have in the past been an Ann Summers representative - this wasn't what I was selling!

This is a simple test, and so if you don't already know the answer, give it a try right now and see what others will find out about you. If you have a website or a landing page and some presence (in the area you want to be known in) that's great news. Other people can see you exist (to be more precise, they can see you exist online) and whilst that is a start, it isn't enough because there are still 2 more elements.

LIKE

Now you can be seen, the next question is, do they like you?

So many of the coaches and consultants that I work with tell me that they can help EVERYONE with their services and products! Which is great…not!

Because unless you have a large marketing budget, you won't be able to reach all these people and when it comes to being "liked" by everyone, the message you put out there would have to be so "middle of the road" as to not to offend anyone, it runs the risk of potentially resonating with no-one either.

The good news is that you can use this information to be seen in an already well-established sector. In fact, using this can even increase your message / attract a new target market, when you know who they are and what they want.

Harvard Business Review stated: trying to "be all things to all people" can backfire, marketers often target a specific consumer segment. In some cases, such segmentation increases polarisation, which in turn can boost revenue.

This played out in the UK market for alcoholic cider. For centuries cider has been consumed much as beer is served without ice, often in working-class pubs.

In 2006 sales of "Magners", a popular brand, soared after a promotional campaign touted it as a refreshing iced summer beverage. The ads helped turn Magners into a hip drink for young upscale professionals, a demographic that hadn't consumed much cider in the past.

The most effective brands create polarisation. Creating a distinction between the people that love them, really, really love them and the people that hate them, well, who cares, I mean that in a way that you can't please all of the people, all of the time and it's probable they were never the right fit anyway.

In the example above, those who don't like cider (ice or no ice) don't like cider! This makes it easy to understand why the industry wouldn't waste its time and money trying to market to everyone. You might be thinking but Cheryl I CAN help everyone with their health, wellbeing, mindset, and business!

Let's test this out:

If I asked you to remember a client that was a 'nightmare,' you'll potentially remember the way

- They "haggled" on price at the start
- How demanding they were throughout
- The one you gave more time to than anyone
- And yet they still weren't happy.

Yep, you guessed it, they weren't really for you. Perhaps you needed money at the time, or you didn't know who your target client was and so you tried to help everyone.

So, when I say not the right fit for you, this may be that they just didn't resonate with you or even value you, although you could help them, they didn't want to put the time, energy, and money into being helped, so in essence they were not the right client for you.

Does that make sense?

To get your client to give you attention, there's just one thing you need to do.

Be yourself.

That's really it.

The reality is, even if you try to be someone else, you may still have. your supporters (who like the image you're portraying) and those who don't resonate with you (or the image you're trying to portray) and if you're trying to be someone you're not, that's hard work!

I remember when I first started public speaking – I had been on stage, and I was playing the recording back to my husband. Picture this, I'm sitting there feeling rather proud of myself, when my Sgt Major husband Chippy (yes, army nickname) says "What's with the voice?"

At this stage you can imagine me saying (as I'm crossing my arms in defence):

"What do you mean? What's wrong with the voice?

That's how one speaks when one is on stage."

Now if you don't know me very well, you'll not know that I have a strong Yorkshire accent and 'one' does not usually use words like 'one' LOL!

However, I'm sitting there feeling all self-righteous.

Clearly, hubby doesn't know anything about public speaking. I'm the one who's spent thousands of pounds and hours training in this area. Don't you just hate it when someone less qualified tries to tell you what to do?

I just ignored him.

Anyway, a few weeks later I'm at the Professional Speakers Academy with the founder Andy Harrington as part of his inner circle of trainers called the A.C.E. (Academy Coaching Executive) Team. I've finished doing my presentation and I'm about to receive some feedback from Andy:

"Chez, great content, and your confidence is growing and yet there's something I can't put my finger on. When you sit next to me, you're all 'Yorkshire Pudding', and when you present, it's like you've got a plum in your mouth"

OMG! I don't know if I feel bad that Andy is giving me this feedback or worse because hubby was right!

Official apology to Mr C, you were right and I'm sorry for ignoring your advice. Over the next few weeks, I had to learn to speak onstage, like I did off stage. It was hard because I'd subconsciously adapted my voice on stage. I had to work out how to replace the 'presenter voice' with my real 'E by Gum voice!'

Why had I done this? Well as I look back now, I guess it was fear of judgement and yet it was this change that didn't resonate with the people I knew – those that knew the real Cheryl.

2 months later I had just finished presenting to an audience of 500 people at an event in London, when this lady came running up to me:

"Cheryl, I just wanted to say you are soooo inspiring! Until today I thought I was too fat, too old, and too common to do what I wanted to do in my life, but now I've met YOU, I know anything is possible"

Have you ever had a time when you didn't know whether to laugh or cry?

"Ah thank you, I think that's a compliment!"

"Oh Cheryl, that came out a bit wrong. I mean you're so real, so down to earth and you're so authentic, unlike a lot of people on stage who speak like they've got a plum in their mouth."

And there it was - she wanted honest and down to earth and I could do that, because that's who I really am. That's what I became known for, "The Everyday Influencer", the coach and mentor who speaks the truth, the one who will tell you it's your bum that looks big, not the dress or pants and at the same time, I'll guide you to know what to do about it.

Now people know you exist, and they've decided if they like you, here is the final piece in the jigsaw.

TRUST

Think about this; you don't have to believe that the sun will come up in the morning, you just know it will and so that is the truth.

A belief on the other hand is your truth based on your experiences in life. So, it makes sense that what you believe, may not be the same as another person's belief because their experience could be different to yours, right?

Therefore, in order for someone to trust you they need to 'experience you' because getting someone to trust you is more than just knowing you and liking you. Those are critical first steps in the equation.

If you really want to create a business where people buy from you again and again, you need them to trust you implicitly. Trust that you will deliver what you say, trust that you are who you say you are and trust that you have their back.

So how can you build trust based on this information?

I'd like you to do a little exercise to show how this point is true. I'd like you to remember a time when you trusted someone and make a list of all the reasons why you trusted them - just a list of one-word answers.

For example: reliable, caring, great listener, helpful, supportive, honest, committed, happy, etc.

To make this even more effective you can think of a time when you bought something, and it was a pleasurable experience.

I remember when Mr C wanted a new car, and we were looking around all the garages. When we went into the Mini garage, we were greeted with the smile of the salesperson and she asked us lots of questions, made us a cup of tea and then asked if we wanted to test drive the car. She offered to go in the back so I could be in the front and even asked if I wanted to drive too. When we went back later on, she was as receptive and friendly as she had been before and so she was all of the examples above.

Now think of a time when you didn't trust someone and make a list of words again. For example: unreliable, shifty, liar, rude, ignorant, arrogant, self-indulgent, etc.

Again, if you can think of a time when you didn't buy something, or you regretted doing so, this can help with the exercise too. Mine is on the same day as above except this time we went into the Mercedes garage. We had a Mercedes at the time and despite having done business with that garage before, we were ignored - not even a hello! We walked around as if we were invisible and when we eventually spoke to someone, it was obvious they were not interested at all, so we left. And (you guessed it) we went and bought a mini!

Here's the interesting thing. Because of that, it is highly unlikely that we would go to the Mercedes garage again. Because of the inconsistency. Which leads me quite nicely into 3 elements required to build trust. The first part is you need to be CONSISTENT and have consistency with everything you do. Your clients should have a similar experience with you every single time they deal with you (and your business) unlike the Mercedes garage.

Next comes CONNECTION. When people meet you, they should immediately get a sense of trust. Do they 'feel' you are trustworthy?

Do you ensure they feel cared for, acknowledged and seen? Do they resonate with your energy?

Another area is of course COMMUNICATION. This goes back to the 'know' factor. It is more effective when you communicate in a variety of ways face to face (when you can) and online via video so they can see and hear you and experience you in a multitude of ways. This is because we all have a preferred way of communication. Some prefer visual, others auditory, and for others it is kinaesthetic.

You can often tell a person's preference when you are having 2-way communication as they will say things in a particular way, for example:

Visual "When I saw what they were doing, I just knew I could trust them" or "I prefer to meet face to face, so I can see the other person."

Auditory "I was listening to what they were saying, and the words resonated with me" or "I love the sound of that!"

Kinaesthetic "I just felt a connection between us" or

"I couldn't help but feel safe in her presence." Now you might be thinking, how can I find this out and how can I connect when we can't even meet in person? The key is this, ensure you cover all aspects. Through video you connect visually and auditorily and because they can see and hear you, the viewer gets a sense of how they feel around you too - excellent!

You cover them all and they resonate with the one that suits them best.

Armed with these techniques you can be confident at presenting, as yourself.

CHAPTER 3

Trust In Yourself

Here's what I have found in my capacity as a speaker and mentor with entrepreneurs, employees and enlightened clients all over the globe and that is that one of the biggest barriers other amazing humans have (and I'm sorry ladies it's more so with my female clients) is that they don't trust themselves!

What do I mean by 'not trusting themselves?'

I hear clients say these words all the time:

Who will listen to me?

Who do I think I am?

Do I know enough?

Am I enough?

Will anyone pay for what I know?

What if people mock me?

At least these are questions as the ever more debilitating words are the statements that people say to themselves as if they are true (remember the truth about the sun coming up every day):

I will never be able to share my message

I could never stand up and speak

I am not worthy

I don't know enough to be seen as an expert

I need to learn more skills

Here's the thing, your mind is always listening to you.

When I decided I wanted to help others to overcome these limiting beliefs', I trained as an Advanced Rapid Transformational Therapist. I learned from the amazing Marisa Peer, who developed The R.T.T. Strategy, that the mind is only designed to do 3 things:

a. Keep your safe
b. Seek familiarity
c. Do what it thinks you want it to do

For example, when you say I will never be able to share my message/product/service, your mind says "OK, so let me help you make this true" and on any occasion you think, "well maybe I'll give it a go," your mind remembers what you said and goes into self-preservation mode. Therefore, it creates a 'get out of jail free cards', such as a stutter, excessive sweating, the ability to distract yourself with anything other than speaking and it can even help you to make excuses!

I remember when Aisha, one of the members of The Find Your WHY Foundation group, first put herself forward to do one of the WHYs Words presentations. She was excited and, even though she was not a trained speaker, and she didn't have anything to sell, she just wanted to share her thoughts and ideas and, if you like, create a legacy in the form of videos that could be shared with her family and generations to come.

She was ready and committed to take the actions needed and then her mind kicked in. This is the text she sent me, the day after she had said "Yes, I'm ready"

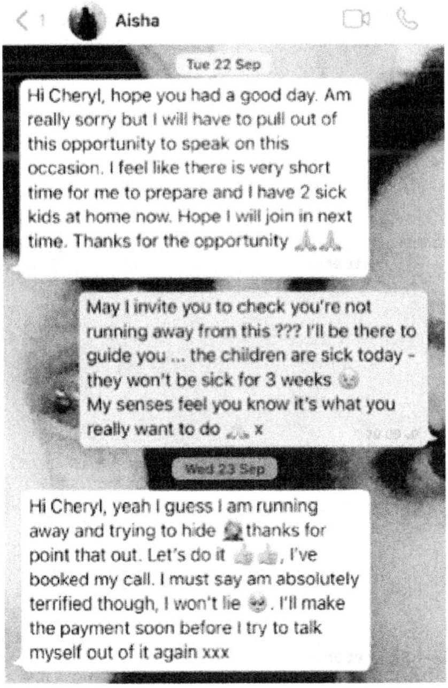

Luckily, I'd been working with Aisha and so I already knew some of her distracting patterns - maybe you know what yours are? I didn't just accept what her mind was saying, which was obviously just an excuse.

When Aisha realised it was just her natural fear kicking in, we began to work on her message (her desire to help other women in her culture) This became her driver. She recorded videos for me to provide feedback, implemented the changes, and she practised.

Here is the text she sent me after her 1st 'dress rehearsal' presentation to fellow speakers:

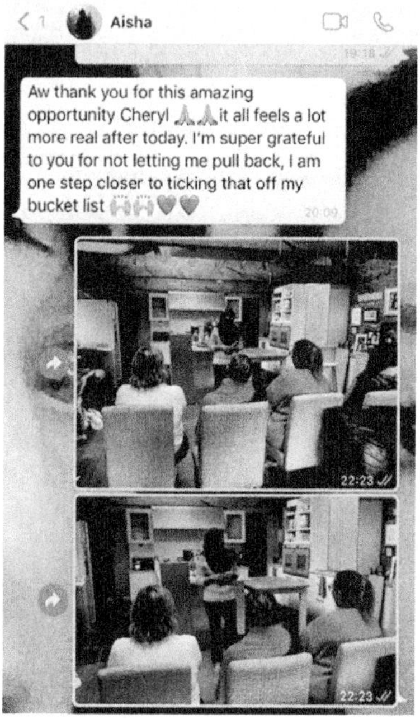

In just 4 weeks after initially saying "Yes", Aisha delivered her professional presentation, where there was not a dry eye in the house, and I interviewed her about her passion to support other women. Here is her story and the links to her videos - enjoy!

Aisha Aminu is originally from Nigeria in West Africa. She is married with three children. She is a team leader at work, a public speaker and is currently training to become a coach and learning about NLP (Neuro-Linguistic Programming). She is also a member of The Find Your Why Foundation where she continues to gain so much confidence, tools, and techniques to help her step into her own power, passion, and purpose. She's always looking to develop herself through learning, attending events and networking. She loves to learn new concepts and is always studying new courses and programmes to enhance her skills, knowledge and understanding.

Personal Development is hugely important to her, i.e. learning to grow and evolve. In life, she has experienced many triumphs and challenges. However, she has a strong faith and is a great believer that everything in life happens for a reason. She fervently believes that God, in his infinite wisdom, has control over everything - nothing is wrong or broken, and we are loved and supported. She uses her learning and experiences in life to fuel her passion, which is helping people reconnect with their authentic self and lead a more fulfilling life. Her definition of a fulfilled life is one where your success is not determined by your titles, whether they are those that we attach to ourselves, or others attach to us. We acquire different titles as we go through life. Some empower us, and some can confine us and hold us back. The most important thing is that they are not there to define who we are and to limit us, but to inspire us to learn, grow and fulfil our own true potential.

Here is the interview I did recently with Aisha at The Live Love Laugh Lives.

If you prefer to watch the video, please use this link:
https://youtu.be/h4s4HBnoL1c

Aisha I'm honoured to be here with you today, to have a chat and share with you some things I've been through and things I've learnt that have really helped me along the way.

Cheryl What is it Aisha that you have been recently sharing and talking about, as you have just started being a speaker, and sharing your thoughts and ideas?
What are some of these that you can discuss with us?

Aisha I'm passionate about trying to get people to understand that they don't have to let labels, being put into certain boxes and pigeonholes, define who they are. You can have titles and roles but still, be yourself. What do I mean by labels? Well, I can be a 'mum', but still have my own identity. It's not all of who I am. I do not have to try to fit into predicted pre-existing conditions of being a mum. I can do it my own way.

Cheryl If someone gives you a label, is that because they've got some kind of preconceived idea of how you should be a mum - of what is right and wrong? Almost like a set way to do it that you are expected to follow.

Aisha Yes, definitely, what I'm trying to do is to get people to understand that you can be a mum and still keep your authenticity and identity. You don't have to be a particular kind of mum. Because you can be the best and happiest mum just by being yourself and enjoying the process without all that added pressure.

Cheryl Have you had a time personally where you felt like you lost who you really were amidst the busyness of motherhood? Is that why you're so passionate about this topic?

Aisha 100%. I was worried about how many labels and expectations I had upon me and what people thought of me and how I was matching up. I was always worrying about how I might come across or how I was doing in comparison with other people.

And whilst living like this and trying to fill so many roles, I found myself in a place where I no longer liked myself. I didn't know who I was anymore, and I was really not enjoying the experience. I wasn't really enjoying being a mum and I didn't have the time to spend with my kids. I was too busy running around trying to tick all the boxes and feel like I was doing and being enough.

Cheryl What advice would you give to people who may be feeling exactly the same as you were? Like they've got way too many labels thrust upon them or they don't feel like they're being themselves anymore? They have got a little lost along the way. What techniques do you now have and could share with other people to help them with this?

Aisha I would say three things. One is that labels will always exist and be there. There will always be opinions and expectations of others, but this does not have to become your truth and dictate your life. It's about bringing your authentic self to the table and being real and true to yourself. It's about you, deciding and defining the title and label you want because it's who you are and not the other way around. Not you are becoming who you feel you need to be or should be. Number two is about giving up control - not always having to feel you have to have a set plan, outcome or answer. We really don't have control over anything except how we choose to respond to the moment. So why try and get ourselves so stressed, overwhelmed and unhappy?

Number three, just try to relax and enjoy your precious life. The only label you need to worry about is yourself - who am I?

To be the best version of you because no one else can do it like you and then those around you get the very best you as you are truly present with them.

Cheryl Yes, that's very true and when you know who you are and are simply being yourself then it can really help everyone else and free them up to do the same. If we all lived our lives just being who we are without comparing and judgement, then we could all stop thinking and worrying about it. It would no longer be an issue having to question if we were getting it right according to another's idea or perception of us. That's the real win-win here for everyone.

So, let's talk about work Aisha, and I think I'm right in thinking that you work with mainly women? Would that be a fair comment?

Aisha Yeah, it's mainly women from my background, which is one of an ethnic minority. It's another reason I feel it's so important for me to share as I want people to understand that you don't have to fit into what other people may think of you or how you should be. No matter what, you have the right to be yourself and live up to your own title of being the best version of you which comes from within.

Cheryl To give you some labels so we know a little more about you on a surface level. You are a mum, a working woman, a graduate, you're a busy bee! So, what happened to you for you to realise that all these labels were getting in your way? Because a lot of people go through life thinking that they are their titles, and they forget who they are underneath all that. There is a lack of understanding and awareness that these labels can be really affecting them negatively as they are striving and trying so hard to please somebody else. So, what was it specifically that made you realise what was happening for you and had you thinking differently?

Can you remember?

Aisha I think my turning point was when we got a diagnosis for my son. He was fourteen and out of nowhere he got diagnosed with cancer. At that moment, I lost control over anything that I thought I ever had control over. The only thing I had left to depend on was to simply let go, breathe and be myself. To simply be present there with my family in love. So, afterwards, I thought to myself 'why go back to the way I was living before?' It all felt so meaningless and for all the striving I realised that really, we have no control over the things that truly matter. It made me face the truth that I cannot fit into a label that isn't meant for me and that I didn't want to for a moment longer.

Cheryl The story of what you went through with your son is so very moving. If people want to watch and find out more about that, then they can obviously go and watch it for themselves. It can be seen on YouTube under the WHYs Words channel. It's very heartfelt, honest, and raw, so thank you for sharing that. It really did show the authentic you as you share what you were going through at the time when you felt out of control in the situation. It's a really lovely piece to listen to, even though it's admittedly not about a very happy subject and was a difficult time. But you stepped up and were very brave which is admirable. We will let people go and view it for themselves as I don't want to give too much away! So, to change the tone now slightly, what do you like to do for yourself on a day to day basis in your life now?

Aisha I do still have some labels, as we all do. I am a mum of three, and I'm working full time again but I've made some really simple but vital changes in my daily routine. The first thing I do when I wake up in the morning is set my intention to remember to always be myself and to be the best version of me. To not worry about what other people think and get bogged down with that. Of course, I do fall into some of those traps every now and then - I'm only human. But I don't beat myself up as I think the key is awareness. When

you find yourself slipping back into that, you simply bring yourself back as quickly and gently as you can. I now know that true fulfilment is not comparing yourself with others, not trying to fit into what other people think, not worrying about what they expect of you.
So, every single day I try to be the best version of me and be present with my loved ones and that makes me feel like I'm loving and honouring my true self.

Cheryl I do love that Dr. Seuss quote which says, 'Be you because everyone else is taken'. I think that sums it up brilliantly and simply.
So, Aisha what do you love?
What's your passion?
Obviously, you're passionate about helping other women to drop these labels and to not be confined by them. But what else do you love doing for you? And finally, we are looking at, what makes you laugh?

Aisha I am really enjoying the experience and freedom of just being authentic. The freedom it brings the space and joy to just be me and to be present with whoever I am with. I am very drawn to people who can stand strong in who they are with all their flaws - as we all have them. It inspires me and challenges me to try my best to always be myself with all my friends and family. I also love to see and be around funny people. I love it when people are not trying to be perfect. When you can be with someone who can laugh at life and themselves and not take it all too seriously, it really is a tonic. It's a great place to be in when you can know that in life you either win, lose or learn and that's OK. So, I make sure that every single day I laugh with my kids. I find something that is funny. Laughter feels good and we should all do more of it.

Cheryl Yes, we really should. It's part of our motto for a reason - to Live, Love and Laugh every day is a winning combination. Aisha, thank you so much for sharing your thoughts, your wisdom and your authenticity with us today, i'm sure it will help and inspire many others.

Reach out to Aisha and find out more about her.
aishaminu@yahoo.co.uk
www.facebook.com/aisha.bashir.54

See Aisha sharing her presentation in October 2020 via this YouTube link:
https://youtu.be/v9OFP4AApEY

"Living Authentically Without Labels"

The truth is that in trying to keep you safe, your mind can talk you out of the very acts which would help you to live your life and create a legacy long after you have gone.

Aisha now has these videos to share with her family. Showing her daughter her presentation brought a deep connection as her daughter said, "I didn't realise how difficult it was for you."

Interestingly, Aisha has also found her voice at work and is now speaking out to help her team and the organisation she works for. If you resonate with Aisha's situation, I'd love to find out if you would like to leave a legacy and how I can help you get your message out to those who need it.

The first thing you can do is connect with me by sending an email to *cheryl@cheryl-chapman.com* with the title "I want to be a more confident speaker"

"It is impossible to live without failing at something unless you live so cautiously that you might as well not have lived at all in which case you fail by default."

J.K. Rowling

The question is, of course, how can you overcome this built in 'lifesaver' that will try to keep you so safe that you don't really live your life to the fullest? And is it even important to trust in yourself enough to change?

The answer, of course, is yes because if you don't trust you, how can you expect anyone else to? It is imperative that you recognise that you know enough to help someone.

The reason why you might not, can be for so many reasons.

A lot of our limiting beliefs (beliefs that hold you back from your potential) come from our formative years, learned from well-meaning parents, teachers, and people of influence around you.

They are usually based on the ones they themselves learned at an early age too, and so the limiting belief cycle goes on.

There are many books on the many techniques that can be used to help you in this area. However, in essence, it's about changing the words you say to yourself and the pictures you make in your mind.

I'd like you to do this simple exercise:

1. **What is your limiting belief?**
   e.g., *I don't think I know enough to help others.*

2. **Now what comes into your mind when you write this down? What is the picture in your mind?**
   e.g., *I can see a crowd of people in front of me all laughing and joking with each other, pointing a finger at me, and saying "who does she think she is?"*

3. **What are the words you are saying?**
   e.g., *They are all laughing at me, they think I'm stupid, why did I ever think this would work, I don't know enough to help anyone.*

4. **How are you feeling?**
   e.g., *I'm feeling embarrassed and ashamed.*

5. **When was the first time you ever had this feeling in your life – how old were you and what was happening?**
   e.g., *When I was at school about 11 years old and I was reading from a book and I said a word wrong, the children in the class and the teacher were laughing at me.*

6. **What action did you want to / did take?**
   e.g., *I went red and wanted to run away, I was fighting back the tears and when the lesson was over, I ran home and cried*

7. **Now write down all the reasons why you are not that same person (as the first time you had this feeling)**
   e.g., *This isn't me now because I'm no longer 11 years old. This isn't me now because I don't stand up and read to a class, this is no longer me because if someone was laughing at me, I'd just say, give me a chance and stop laughing.*

8. **Create an image of you doing the "thing" you put down under question number 1.**
   e.g., *I'm standing in front of a room of people and reading from a book, I have practised the chapter and so I am very familiar with the words. The words are flowing from my mouth and the audience is smiling and enjoying the words and the way I am delivering the information from the page.*

9. **How are you feeling?**
   e.g., *I'm feeling happy and calm.*

10. **Add some positive intention words**
    e.g., *I am enjoying the experience of sharing the information that I have to the audience, and they are loving it too. It is becoming easier and effortless with every word.*

11. **What action do you want to take?**
    e.g., *I want to do this again* ☺

This is all based on Neuro-Linguistic Programming (NLP).

NLP is a psychological approach that relates thoughts, language, and patterns of behaviour learned through experience to specific outcomes. From a high-level overview this means the following:

When a piece of information comes into your mind, it equals a thought (**Neuro**) and to decide what to do with this information the mind either.

- Deletes it (not of importance right now). According to Britannica.com the body sends 11 million bits per second to the brain for processing and the conscious mind only seems to be able to process 50 bits per second. That's a lot of compression/deletion going on right?
- Duplicates it (relates it to something familiar) For example, when you come across a door, even if you've never seen it before, your mind says "oh yeah this is like all those other 'doors'" and goes ahead and uses the information it knows to open it.
- Distorts it (a piece of information is taken for what it isn't and made into something else).

There are 5 ways to do this and one of them is "mind reading" e.g., I know what you are thinking when you look at me like that! I have to say the first time I heard of NLP; I thought it was a London car parking system because in the North of England we have NCP (National Car Parking).

So, I thought NLP was National London Parking!

Can you see how my mind used the duplication to relate to something I already knew and at the same time it distorted it? Once you get a thought and go through this process, you'll be seeing images and saying words to yourself (hence the exercise I asked you to do earlier with images and words)

This is the **Linguistic** part of NLP.

Finally, based on this, you will behave in a certain way, and you will act. This will be based on a number of additional elements such as your previous experiences, habits and what you've been taught.

This is the P of NLP, which is **Programming**. Depending on this programming, you may decide to act by doing a positive action, doing the wrong action, reacting (as opposed to responding, so it tends to have a negative action, as it's done in the moment) or doing nothing (inaction).

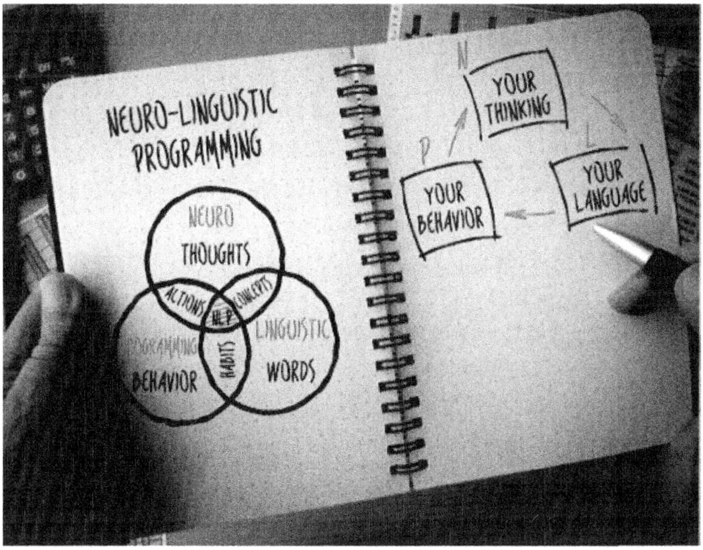

I have been working with people in the information sharing space for over 10 years and I've noticed one startling thing. The smarter someone is (in the sense of being educated) the more they seem to doubt themselves.

They may have terrific experience and incredible judgment, but they appear to have the knowledge that they'll never know everything there is to know even about their favourite subjects.

As Socrates said

"The more I learn, the less I realise I know"

Less-capable, less-curious people appear to doubt themselves much less. I remember talking to a woman who had her own beauty business. She was streetwise and when I spoke to her about all the things that could go wrong in her business (yes, this was before my own self-development journey), she just said "well, if it does, I'll just do something else."

It reminded me of being a child and going on all the rides at a fun fair - just there enjoying the ride! Interesting, as you get older and 'wiser' it's then that you might start thinking about the crash possibilities and what might go wrong (or was that just me?).

Recently, I went to Florida, and I went on every ride I could, saying to myself "I love these rides". And guess what? I did. It all goes back to the mind listening in and doing what it thinks you want. Every day, you can influence your mind and of course others too.

I talk to everyday influencers every day. I am amazed by their stories, their observations, and their wisdom. People say that every person has a book in them waiting to come out, and many people have more than one book in them! However, very few go ahead and write one, stating they don't know enough, or they don't know how to do it, or they don't have time.

They are happy to help anybody solve their problems, but they may still be hesitant when the time comes to talk about themselves. I recently introduced a "Brag-off" in the WHYs women community, so I could see how many would share their successes. Here is what Helen Bartram, crowned WHYs Woman of the year for 2019, said:

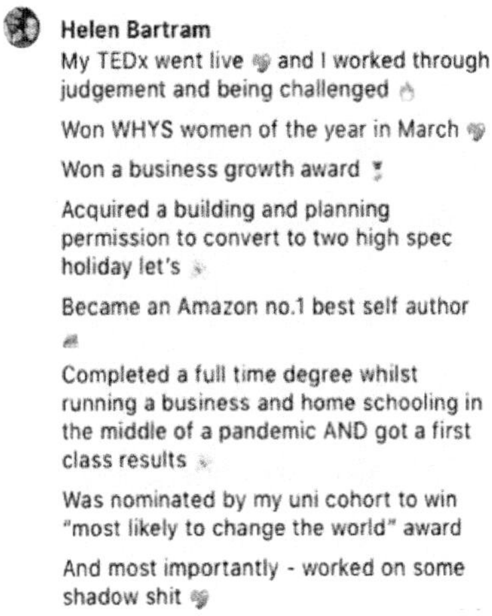

Helen Bartram
My TEDx went live and I worked through judgement and being challenged

Won WHYS women of the year in March

Won a business growth award

Acquired a building and planning permission to convert to two high spec holiday let's

Became an Amazon no.1 best self author

Completed a full time degree whilst running a business and home schooling in the middle of a pandemic AND got a first class results

Was nominated by my uni cohort to win "most likely to change the world" award

And most importantly - worked on some shadow shit

Here is the interesting addition to this post:

Helen Bartram
I'm adding to my list cause I never bloody brag and I'm not comfortable with it so I'm going all out while I'm here ha :

- was interviews on bbc radio

- launched a new business - happiness coach

- wrote a programme to launch in 2021

- became an accredited training school and had 5 courses accredited and people booked on for 2021

- launched a podcast

- was invited to be a monthly contributor to a magazine

- recorded and launched a children's mental health online programme

- qualified in EFT

Even when she was aware of all the achievements, she was also still aware of the feeling of not being comfortable with the "brag-off" concept. Why? Maybe as a child she was told to "stop showing off"? It is these 'beliefs and rules that can hold you back, until you learn that, in order to help others, you need to show what your achievements are. To be clear, this is not about you introducing yourself to every new person you meet as The XYZ Expert. You can, however, say what you do and who you help and then, of course, they can decide for themselves.

We decided Helen was an everyday influencer and that's why she was crowned our WHY's Woman of the Year 2019. She knows enough about how to turn around your thoughts and that is why she is now known as 'The Happiness Coach'. Well done, Helen!

Her TEDxAinleyTopWomen Talk has also been watched over 7k times.

It reminds me of another everyday influencer, Joanne Ingram, she is a survivor of narcissism, that almost cost her life. I'm sure you would agree she may have some wisdom to share around that, to help others avoid or get away from a similar situation.

When we were working on her presentation for the Confidently Come Speaking event, I became aware of her reluctance to share all of her achievements, and this is where the story came to light. By working with Joanne to help her express her results, she was able to deliver a presentation that truly positioned her as the guide she is to support and help others in their transformation. Joanne is a quiet, almost shy woman and yet when she is sharing her wisdom, it's like she comes alive.

Here is the interview I did with Joanne at the Confidently Come Speaking Event You can read it here or copy the links to watch the interview and her presentation to find out more about who she really is and what she does for her clients.

If you prefer to watch the video, please use this link:
https://youtu.be/YrAfOqAo6eA

INTRODUCING AWARD WINNING INTERNATIONAL SPEAKER & EVERYDAY INFLUENCER

Joanne Ingram

Joanne has lived a truly extraordinary and diverse life. Throughout her journey, Joanne has encountered a plethora of experiences that encompass both joy and pain.

These life events have shaped Joanne's character and fuel a personal transformation that radiates strength and resilience. With a deep-rooted passion for empowering women, she is dedicated to helping others thrive and unleash their full potential. Here is the interview I did with Joanna at the July 2023 Speaking Event.

Cheryl Today, I'm joined by an incredible fellow Yorkshire speaking, amazing woman and so, I'm just going to ask you to introduce yourself.

Joanne Hi, my name's Joanne Ingram, and I help people with their health and well-being.

Cheryl I remember the first time that we met Joanne, you were like, oh, there's no way I'm ever going to be on the stage, and I was like, oh, well, we might be able to help you with that. Have you got a message? and you said, yeah, I've got a message. So, do you want to share a little bit about what you do to help people in their health and well-being?

Joanne Yes- so, I have a clinic in Barnsley and it's a cryotherapy clinic where I offer various treatments. So, I started out offering cryotherapy and then I went into massage and then sports massage and a few different holistic treatments.

Cheryl What is cryotherapy?

Joanne Cryotherapy is ice therapy; it is where extreme cold temperatures are produced with liquid nitrogen. So, I offer targeted cryotherapy, which is mainly for injuries and pain and then whole-body cryotherapy as well as treating injuries in pain. It helps with a whole number of other issues. So, it helps with improving sleep, inflammation, anxiety, and depression, improves mood, improves immunity, and has a whole host of benefits, whole body benefits.

Cheryl And you were saying to me the other day when we were just chatting, you were saying that what happened was most people were coming to this place, for body ailments and then a little bit like a hairdresser, they started to talk to you. What sort of things would they share with you?

Joanne Yeah, well, I offer some women's specific treatments as well, and it's quite intimate, so you get talking. And I could kind of sense that a lot of these women were having other issues in their life, and they talked to me about some of the problems they were facing. So, it kind of became apparent that there was some emotional trauma or some issues that they were trying to deal with but couldn't quite deal with on their own.

Cheryl Yeah, yeah, it's kind of like you can't take your own appendix out so maybe they needed some help and support in that area. And I know you were on stage quite recently, so yes! for being on stage and sharing your message. But obviously, in that story, I remember there was a bit where you'd been doing bodybuilding because you'd get yourself in shape and you were sort of pushing yourself into new areas. I think you said that your friend was in the audience, and you just said you were just trying to push yourself through. Why were you trying to do that?

Joanne "Well, I'd always been shy, quiet, and I wanted to improve my confidence. I had experienced some bad relationships and I knew I had to change my life. And one of the first things I did was start my fitness journey which then led to bodybuilding."

Cheryl "I'm aware you did share something, I don't know how to quite put it because it sounded like such a horrific time in your life, but you didn't have just one problematic relationship you had a few, didn't you? If you don't mind sharing, what were one of the "worst, darkest moments that you had in those relationships?

Joanne Um, where my first relationship was quite violent and at one point I was strangled and to the point of being unconscious and I thought I wouldn't see my children again. And I really didn't know how to escape from that because I tried to leave several times, but I was stalked. And it was only when he finally went to prison that I managed to kind of start afresh but then I fell victim to a narcissist.

Cheryl "Well. Good choices, not!"

Joanne "No, no."

Cheryl "Narcissism is a big topic right now, isn't it? You know, you see on social media."

Joanne "Yeah

Cheryl And I guess one of the questions that people may have asked you or they might question, you know, even if they're not sort of brave enough to ask the person who's been through it is, well why would you even stay in a relationship like that? I mean, you might be shy, but you know, you look like you can look after yourself. What's it like being in a relationship with a narcissist?

Joanne When I met him, I didn't have any self-confidence, and he appeared to be this wonderful human being who was very charming, very strong, very good-looking and he pursued me. And I think now I know they call it Love Bombing and at the time, I didn't know what kind of relationship I was in. I knew it was very difficult, but I had no idea that it was an abusive relationship until it finished. I tried, you know, a lot of times to get out, but he threatened to kill himself, and it was just difficult. I was just so confused. I didn't know what had gone wrong from this charming man to this monster, really. But there were high points, and there were low points. But the low points outweighed the highs so, I knew I had to leave.

Cheryl So, you went on a journey of self-discovery, and self-empowerment and now, of course you're helping other women to overcome adversity in their relationships and lives. how do you do that?

Joanne Yes. So, I created 'The Best Version of You Blueprint', that's the name of it. It's basically the journey that I went through myself When I left those two relationships, I would say I was in despair. I didn't know how to make my life better, but I knew kind of deep down inside that there had to be more to life than what I had already experienced. Because that took me from kind of my late teens right up to being almost 40, those two relationships. I desperately wanted my life to get better, so I embarked on this journey, as I say. First, it was in fitness, and then the fitness gave me the confidence to do other things, and it kind of progressed from there.

Cheryl And you're a great role model for anybody who feels like they're stuck, doesn't feel enough. You know, you still have nerves now, before you were getting on stage, you were like, oh my gosh, you know, I'm going to be able to do this. But what I really love about you, Joanne, is that you look, you take something, and you go, I don't know if I can do it, but you know what?

I'm going to put everything into it. I'm going to practice; I'm going to rehearse. I'm going to find a way out of that. It's almost like you were controlled for so long that now you've taken back the control of your life, does that resonate?

Joanne Yeah. I was desperate to make my life better, and I would do anything to make it better, I would try anything.

Cheryl And I know in your talk, you talk about how you read lots of books. For example, you referred to The Secret, and how you're still looking for the secret…it's well hidden, isn't it? And so, if anybody else wanted to find out a bit more about how to work with you, where would they be able to get in contact with you?

Joanne So, I'm on Facebook under Cryotherapy Barnsley, and I've also got a website which is www.CryotherapyBarnsley.co.uk and I'm on Instagram as well, but mainly through those two mediums.

Cheryl Great., we'll pop the links below so that you can connect with Joanne. And I just want to say, I just thank you for being so incredible, inspiring and amazing. Breaking through those barriers, you know, even when you were in the real depths of despair and like you said, you didn't even know whether you were going to live or die.

So, breaking through that, coming back stronger and becoming the person that you were born to be. So, thank you so much for sharing your story, your journey, and obviously helping more people to get out of that situation.

Joanne Thank you.

Cheryl Thank you so much for listening. If you'd like to find out more about Joanne, we'll put the links below. And if you'd like to see her talk, then we'll put the link in there so you can find out a little bit more about some funny sides of her life, as well as some of the serious ones. We'll see you soon, so remember to stand up and keep speaking out.

See Joanne sharing her wisdom at the Live Confidently Come Speaking 2023 via this
YouTube link: *https://youtu.be/YrAfOqAo6e*

It is all about getting the balance right; being able to be seen, heard and felt so others can get to know, like and trust you in a way that isn't perceived as showing off.

All whilst avoiding being the world's best kept secret!

There is another way that you can help others to know how amazing you are and that is to let other people brag about you. If you think about celebrities, they are often in the media or on chat shows where the host is the one positioning them.

Being interviewed helps to position you as a person of interest - someone who is being called on to share their opinion and, therefore, someone with some experience in that area. People will often be introduced as a specialist, expert or mentor, which of course immediately elevates them, without them having to blow their own trumpet, so to speak!

Since standing on stage Joanne has been approached to do many talks with local businesses.

CHAPTER 4

The Process

In order to be seen as an Everyday Influencer, there is a process. The truth is most entrepreneurs usually get into business because they love what they do but rarely are they trained to speak in public. This means in order for people to know, like and trust them, it is a case of knowing the following 5 areas to avoid being a faceless wonder!

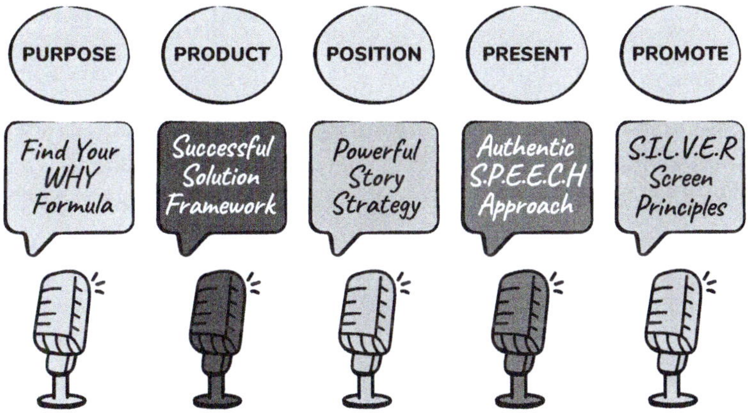

THE CONFIDENT SPEAKER SYSTEM™

PURPOSE

If you don't know why you want to share your knowledge, whether that be in the form of a product, service or just guidance, the chances are that you'll give up at the first hurdle. It is also true that when you have a purpose, it's the reason to get out of bed, even on those days when you just want to snooze the alarm!

There is something about someone who lives their life with purpose, determination, and the desire to succeed, that makes them attractive - someone to follow. So, it makes sense that if you do not have this, you can miss out on attracting those you can serve.

Later on, in the next chapter I'll share with you the way you can start to find your true purpose. Purpose is a 'must-have', although it's not the only thing you need in order to become a Freedom Speaker or Everyday Influencer because you also need to have a PROPOSAL.

PRODUCT

What do I mean by a product?

It's what you have that is knowledge, an experience that you have been through that you know can help others with.

If you don't have a product or service just yet and you do want one, there is 1 thing that I can share with you straight away. It is possible for you to already have enough information and life experiences to help others.

So many of my clients feel like they don't know enough to start serving others and so I'm telling you, if you are an adult (and what I mean by that is you've had some hard knocks in life, in areas of health, wealth, relationships, or business, for example) then you have learned some lessons, right? So, when it comes to a proposal for an Everyday Influencer, it's not about how many millions you've made or how many degrees you've got, and it's not about climbing Mount Everest.

It's about how you overcame the 'mountain' that you climbed, to deal with the death of a loved one. Overcoming the disappointment when you didn't get a promotion, or when someone left you are feeling deserted. And more recently, when there was a disaster, like Covid-19, and you found a way to stay sane and stable. This is what everyday people are looking for because do you know where they go right now? Potentially, they go to the soaps - that's right '*Deadenders*' and '*Crapanation Street*'. Why? Because here they find people in the same situation as themselves or even worse and so, by comparison, they feel better. The truth is, all that happens there is that they potentially get stuck in the belief that their life is not as bad as someone else's, and they settle for a good life and not a fulfilled one.

This is where you come in, because if you know your PURPOSE and your PRODUCT then you are able to do what you love, help others and receive a positive exchange (e.g.,money!). I'll talk more about that later.

These are great places to start and now it's about taking your PURPOSE and PRODUCT and moving to the next stage, because if you don't, well your audience may not know you are the right person to help them.

This is all about how to POSITION yourself, as the go to person.

POSITION

If you want someone to listen to you, you need to position yourself.

Not in a Brenda big boobs, or Billy big bollocks, showing off in a look at me sort of way.

However, I'm sure you would agree there has to be a way of showing the audience that you do know what you're talking about.

Now we start to look at how you can present all the previous 3 areas. In the best way, you need to know how to PRESENT and be present with your audience.

PRESENT

In terms of PRESENT, I mean how can you share what you know to others? There are many ways to engage the senses: written word, spoken word and of course visually (on video or in person). To be a sensational speaker, of course, the latter can incorporate so many of the senses - vision, hearing, smell, touch and to include a 6th sense of 'gut instinct' or 'intuition' about someone. Therefore, it is the one I believe that can connect you to someone else in a quicker and more sensitive way!

However, speaking in public is known to be the number 1 fear for many humans. According to Brandon Gaille, 75% of people experience some degree of anxiety or nervousness when public speaking, and 10% of people are terrified. Speaking in public is one of the most common fears, ranking among heights, death and snakes.

I'm sure like me, you may have experienced some sort of fear when speaking in public at some time in your life. Yes, I've been there with the dry mouth, sweaty palms and what feels like a frontal-lobotomy.

I couldn't remember my name, let alone what to say next! However, a person who is unable to control their nerves and has an extremely strong fear of public speaking, (sometimes to the point of a nervous breakdown) with uncontrollable trembling, sweating, and a racing heartbeat, is said to have Glossophobia.

The term Glossophobia derives from the Greek word γλῶσσα glōssa, meaning tongue, and φόβος phobos, meaning fear or dread. It may not be confined to speaking to large audiences. People suffering with Glossophobia may struggle to speak in a meeting, classroom and in other smaller group settings. This can make it very difficult for sufferers to communicate verbally in order to express their ideas and thoughts. As a result, Glossophobia may hamper their ability to further their academic, social or business opportunities. Some of the reasons behind this fear are:

Natural human response to being expelled

Remember the fear of being forced from the Tribe.

Negative experiences usually early on in life

From negative viewpoints of oneself, such as "nobody cares about what I have to say". This might be caused by a time when you talked in a group situation and were ridiculed for what you said.

Runs in the family

Monkey see – Monkey do and, taking this even further, Monkey don't see – monkey do!

Here is a story originating from research by G.R. Stephenson

The Five Monkey Experiment

An experimenter puts 5 monkeys in a large cage. High up at the top of the cage, well beyond the reach of the monkeys, is a bunch of bananas. Underneath the bananas is a ladder.

The monkeys immediately spot the bananas, and one begins to climb the ladder. As he does, however, the experimenter sprays him with a stream of cold water. Then, he proceeds to spray each of the other monkeys.

The monkey on the ladder scrambles off. And all 5 sit for a time on the floor, wet, cold, and bewildered. Soon, though, the temptation of the bananas is too great, and another monkey begins to climb the ladder. Again, the experimenter sprays the ambitious monkey with cold water and all the other monkeys as well. When a third monkey tries to climb the ladder, the other monkeys, wanting to avoid the cold spray, pull him off the ladder and beat him.

Now one monkey is removed, and a new monkey is introduced to the cage. Spotting the bananas, he naively begins to climb the ladder. The other monkeys pull him off and beat him.

Here's where it gets interesting. The experimenter removes a second one of the original monkeys from the cage and replaces him with a new monkey. Again, the new monkey begins to climb the ladder and, again, the other monkeys pull him off and beat him - including the monkey who had never been sprayed.

By the end of the experiment, none of the original monkeys were left and yet, despite none of them ever experiencing the cold, wet, spray, they had all learned never to try and go for the bananas.

This shows your fear may not even be something you've experienced!

Self-defeating thoughts

Remember your mind is listening and wants to do what it thinks you want to do. It will do anything to keep you safe and that includes minimising change. The situation here is that you will need to PRESENT your ideas, solutions, or products, even if you do have some fears from the above.

The best way to overcome these in the main is to get into action, and the best way to learn to present is to present! I have developed a way to help you to do this, even if you think your voice might shake as much as your knees!

And here's the even better news, even if you are used to speaking in front of others and you don't have any nerves, there is still a way to make you present in an even more effective and efficient way, whilst entertaining the audience. I will share this with you in the coming chapters.

Finally, once you know your PURPOSE, and the PRODUCT you have, you know how to POSITION yourself and how to PRESENT, there is one last thing and this is how to PROMOTE in the best way to be seen, heard and be felt by your audience and potential clients.

PROMOTE

Whilst marketing can be about using adverts and building funnels. Here I'm talking about how to PROMOTE you.

Meaning that when people find your advert, funnel, social media, or website, they get to see, hear and feel you. That's right - it's about how to decrease the time it takes for them to know, like and trust you. Do this wrong or only share text on your website and it's a bit like trying to bake a cake with one ingredient - the proof is in the no-pudding.

Get this right and within a few minutes, your potential client can connect with you and feel like they have known you for a long time.

To guide others to become sensational speakers and Everyday influencers, so they can be seen, heard and felt, I created The

Confident Speaker System, it consists of 5 modules that are designed to help you through the 5 areas of need that I have just introduced to you. I'd like to share these with you in the next chapters. Enjoy!

CHAPTER 5

The W.H.Y. Finder Formula™

To help my clients understand their **PURPOSE**, I Created **The W.H.Y. Finder Formula™**. This is a simple process to help them to understand what they really want to focus on. From the experience of helping hundreds of people like you to Find Your WHY, I know that it helps if you have both the clarity and the confidence to go towards the dreams you want. In this case it's about understanding this specific area of your life and why you want to do this.

This is to reduce the chances that you'll give up at the first hurdle. Let's look at the 3 parts of this process, please go ahead and write down the word WHY.

First things first, if you don't know the person you want to help then you may find yourself being the Jack or Jill to everyone and not connecting to the right people. You therefore need to know Who you want to serve and when I say who, I mean you need to know as much about this person as you can.

Their sex, age, profession, where they live, what car they drive, what magazines they read, hobbies, likes, dislikes, what keeps them awake at night, their fears, and their deepest worries to name but a few. The reason for this is because without this depth of information, you don't really know them and so how can you help them?

The great news is that I find that most of my clients were their own first client. That's right - they want to share what they wished they had known back in the day. Something that they wish someone had shared with them, to avoid the pain they endured or to make it a little less painful. This makes the investigation into your ideal client a bit easier, right?

And if you weren't your first client, what is the common denominator between your most successful clients (the ones you could help the most?) Create an avatar of them, not a blue character from an animated 2009 film, but in fact a representation of your ideal client.

Next the question is: **How** are you going to help your ideal clients? Will you be doing this 1:1 or in small groups? Online or in person? Will it be a service such as therapy, coaching, or mentoring? Or will it be through a product? Do you already have a product or a service? Or do you need to create one? Many of the clients I work with have information and yet they don't know how to share this information in a way that is easily explainable or shown to the people they can help. The reason for this is that most of it is inside their head.

Think about this for a minute. When did you experience the most successful outcome for someone you worked with or someone you helped? You have a picture in your mind, right? Where were you? Who was there? What did they need help with? What did you do? What did they do? What happened after that?

As you are answering my questions. there is a process that you can recall. This, my friend, is how you help people.

I know you might be thinking "but Cheryl, this was just one client, and they are all different, so I would need lots of different processes!" Not true. Yes, there are different responses, but when you look at the process from a higher level, it will be the same.

Let me give you an example:

- Client is in pain
- Client has tried some things which didn't work out
- Client is with you looking for a solution
- You ask about the above
- You provide a solution and client is happy

Notice this could be for health, wealth, happiness, relationships, a house, a car, clothes, or any number of things. Your client doesn't like where they are and so they need a solution, and your process helps them.

Result?

Ideal match!

I help my clients to create a way to deliver this process in a quick and easy way so that their clients can see the solution and therefore, know what is available. This way they see the solution to the problem they have.

The final part of **The W.H.Y. Finder Formula™** is the Y which stands for **Yield** i.e. what is the Yield for you?

What do I mean by this?

I mean what is in it for you Many enlightened souls that I work with say they don't do this for the money. They do this because they just want to help people. And whilst that usually gets a response from me of "great but how are you going to eat?" There is another thought I want to share with you from Marion Bevington, my co-founder at The Find Your WHY Foundation. You might want to write this down:

Nobody does anything for anyone without a gain for themselves.

Think about this, whether it's because you want to help the person, the community, the country or even the world - this will make you feel good, right? Your yield may not be money, but it will give you something in return - and a good feeling is priceless!

However, I'm going back to the question of "how are you going to eat?" I've worked with some poor enlightened souls, who had no way of being able to connect to the people they could serve, and I've worked with those who had a lot more than the wealthy entrepreneurs who were able to connect and serve with them. I remember meeting Marie Diamond, the secret behind 'The Secret' the film which, along with the book of the same name, has reputedly reached over 500 million people.

Rhonda Byrne, the producer of the film and author Rhonda Byrne, the producer of the film and author of the book, is said to be worth $100 million and that is because the movie and the book reached so many people. Interestingly, Marie told me this was the first interview she had ever done and, whilst doing a movie was on her vision board, she didn't get a penny from the film or the book. Today by sharing her wisdom through paid "Law of Attraction" and Feng Shui programs and seminars, she too has created abundance for herself, which I believe to be around $500,000, reached so many people.

Interestingly, Marie told me this was the first interview she had ever done and, whilst doing a movie was on her vision board, she didn't get a penny from the film or the book. Today by sharing her wisdom through paid "Law of Attraction" and Feng Shui programs and seminars, she too has created abundance for herself, which I believe to be around $500,000.

When I met Marie in Prague, I had just finished presenting and she came to talk with me to invite me to join ATL (Association of Transformational Leaders) with her. Have you ever had a time when someone saw you in a way that you didn't see yourself?

I was looking around trying to figure out who she was speaking to! Within 6 months of joining ATL, I became a director, and we quadrupled the membership with other enlightened souls across Europe.

This leads me to a situation and question that comes up for many of my clients which goes something like this.

Who will listen to me? Who would pay me money? Who do I think I am? Ask me how I know about these questions?

There is an amazing poem that I have used and shared that I hope will help you too:

Our Greatest Fear

It is our light not our darkness that most frightens us
Our deepest fear is not that we are inadequate.
Our deepest fear is that we are powerful beyond measure.
It is our light not our darkness that most frightens us.
We ask ourselves, who am I to be brilliant,
gorgeous, talented and fabulous?

Actually, who are you not to be?
You are a child of God.
You're playing small does not serve the world.
There's nothing enlightened about shrinking so that other
people won't feel insecure around you.

We were born to make manifest the glory of
God that is within us.
It's not just in some of us; it's in everyone.
And as we let our own light shine,
we unconsciously give other people
permission to do the same.
As we are liberated from our own fear,
Our presence automatically liberates others.

– Marianne Williamson

Take a moment to write down all the people you know who fit into this category and what traits they have that you admire.

Here is the great news, any trait that you admire in someone else is only because you possess it yourself.

Think about it - how do you know what confidence is unless you have experienced it? Also, traits are not what we are born with - they are learnt.

Maybe you just need a little guidance to practice these, so they become more natural. The other benefit of having a purpose is that confidence kind of oozes out of you. I remember seeing a guy on stage once and when I walked into the room, it just hit me. This guy seems like fun, he's confident and I don't know what he's selling, but I'm buying!

There are many people who say that when they meet someone that just appears to be on a mission, they feel compelled to follow them. By following the Who, How and Yield steps of The Find Your W.H.Y. Formula, you can find the passion from within you that can radiate out to others.

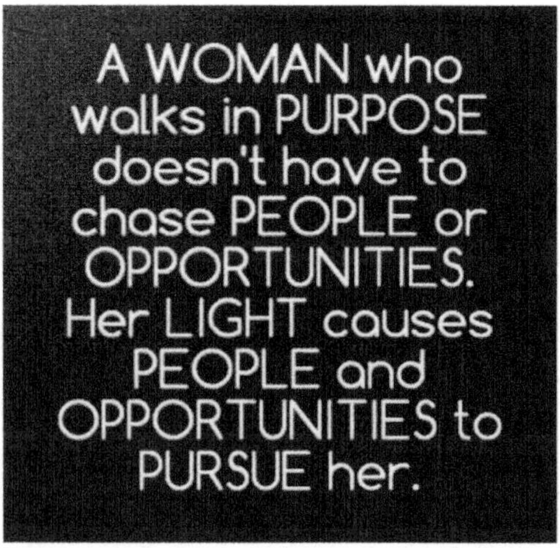

If you would like to see some edutaining (which is education mixed with entertainment) around Finding Your WHY check out this little YouTube video, I made for you:

https://youtu.be/IlH6WVCIQAg

INTRODUCING AWARD WINNING SPEAKER AND EVERY DAY INFLUENCER

Kay Austerberry

Cheryl Hello and welcome, here I'm chatting to WHY's women, women who have found their WHY, their purpose, their passion, and who are sharing their wisdom about what they do in their lives. So today I'm going to ask this amazing lady, I mean, incredible. She's done such a lot in her life, a little bit quirky, shall we say. So, I'm just going to say, who are you and what do you do?

Kay My name is Kay Austerberry, and I'm a Holistic Therapist.

Cheryl Holistic Therapist. So, what's that all about then?

Kay I work on all levels. I work on the mental, emotional, physical & the spiritual side to get people back off their knees. I love helping people that are on their knees or stuck move forward with their lives.

Cheryl Now, recently I saw you on stage. It was International Women's Day, and you were talking about Rising Again like a Phoenix. Oh, my gosh, you must watch this video. It is a comedy genius moment, and educational. I mean, it's just like an eclectic mix of everything that you need to make yourself feel better and to also learn a lot about what Kay does. And so why was the Phoenix important for you to talk about?

Kay Because I've been through a lot in my life. I've got a lot of t-shirts from divorce to losing a child. I've had lots of problems that I've had in the past that I've had to overcome. And that's why I want to share the tools that I have learnt along the way to help people who have hit rock bottom again, and that have been through many problems, because I've been there and got the t-shirts for a lot of them.

Cheryl Yeah, brilliant. And I know that there was a bit of re-light my fire going on in the background, obviously in keeping with that. And you had something that was like a bit of a wand and although we had a little bit of a joke about what that might be, but what was that piece of equipment that you had on stage?

Kay It was an ITeraCare Frequency device. It's the latest in technology for helping heal people. It's brilliant for dealing with physical pain. So, if you got a bad back, bad knees it helps heal the body basically inside and out.

Cheryl And that's by Wanding

Kay By Wanding yeah, it sounds a bit like a hairdryer. Just wave around the body on certain Meridian points, I've had some fantastic results with it. I'm on a personal mission to get it out there in front of everybody because not everybody knows about it.

Cheryl Yeah. So, if you want to find out a little bit more about that, then obviously we'll help you to get in touch with Kay in a little while.

And so, when you talk about mind, body and spirit, Spirit is important to you. And part of your story was about how you got into this. Do you want to just share a little bit with the viewers about what happened?

Kay Yes, I do work with spirit, and I am a working Medium. They help me with my work, they guide me with my clients. I got into it through the Ouija board, and that's part of my story, that's how I learnt about connecting with the spirit world. And then from there on, they've been with me ever since, helping and guiding me and helping guide my clients.

Cheryl it's worth looking at the video, to just hear about the story. Because obviously, you decided that it was not a good idea to be playing with the Ouija board at the beginning, but it did have a dramatic effect on yourself and the people around you, because you know, something happened. We'll not give it away now, just so you go watch the video of course. So, in your work, then, what I find interesting is that you have a bit of an eclectic mix because up until recently you were also doing another type of work, weren't you? What was that?

Kay Yes, I'm a qualified mortgage broker, so I've done mortgage brokering on and off for over 25 years, and now I've realised that we and I mean therapists are really needed out there in the world.

So many people are in turmoil. That's why I'm on a mission to get out there, be seen and let people know what I do so I can help them feel at peace.

Cheryl So, you are from a logical background. Kay often talks and sort of jokes about, "Yes, she does see dead people" and she can help you. And how does spirit come to you? How does it help you to help other people?

Kay They come into guide, so I see spirit and I also hear spirit. Usually, they come in shouting in my right ear, it maybe the person's relative might have come into the room when I am seeing somebody in session. They might be coming in to give guidance or a telling off because they are pretty good at telling people off (in a nice way). They don't always come in, it's not guaranteed, it's just if that person really needs (not wants) that person to come through, then I can convey that message. It's very comforting for people who need healing and support through grief, hearing from their loved one who has passed.

Cheryl And for those people who maybe don't believe in that side because there will be some people, you do also help other people in other ways. I know recently you set up a new community, didn't you? What was that all about?

Kay Yeah, so I started a new walking group now. So, a group of ladies we meet once a week and we go out walking into Nature because I live near Haworth, so we've got some beautiful countryside around there. And we just go for a walk and a talk and have a laugh and have some fun because I think we've all missed the fun side of things with COVID and lockdown, and that's what we started doing recently. This is still developing because I'm going to start creating weight loss groups and other groups, menopause groups for anyone suffering from menopause. We're going to do lots of things, and I can combine it with my hypnotherapy. We could do hypnosis and tapping which is good for weight loss.

Cheryl I know on stage you were doing this tapping. How does that help?

Kay Tapping, that's the Emotional Freedom Technique. It's EFT that's good for phobias. It's good for panic attacks, just like I was having earlier, it's good for cravings, it's very good for all sorts of things

Cheryl Good stuff. And it kind of works on the meridians.

Kay Yes, the meridians

Cheryl If somebody is out there right now, where are they right now? Where they might think that they're not sure if they need help or they do need help, what would you say your ideal client might be potentially going through right now that you can help them with?

Kay A lot of clients that I do attract are people that feel stuck, they feel like stuck in the mud and they just don't know where to go. So, I do another technique called the Emotion Code. That's about releasing emotional baggage, and what that tends to do with clients is it frees their brain and mind up, so they're not full of all this whirring negativity – it calms the mind so that it gives them clear calm space to think. I can then take them forward with what they want to achieve out of life, so we can set goals and intentions for that and use the different tools that I've got in my toolkit, which is massive by the way.

Cheryl Yes. So, I suppose the thing is if you're feeling stuck, you don't really need to know what Kay has got in her tool kit. Just allow her to bring out whatever she needs to and then she can help you to move forward so that you don't feel stuck, and you've got clarity and confidence.

Kay Yeah, exactly.

Cheryl Do you want to just share with people where they can connect with you if they want to find out more?

Kay Yeah, right. My website is *www.kayausterberry.co.uk*. I'm on Instagram and on Facebook and my Facebook business page is Rising Again with Kay, you can find me on that as well. And everything you need to know is on my website.

Cheryl Brilliant. We'll pop those links underneath this video if you want to see Kay on March 11th doing the amazing talk. I mean, honestly, like you'll laugh your cry, you'll be on a rollercoaster of emotions. Then we'll also put the link to that underneath as well. Kay, I want to say thank you so much, not only for being here today, not only for standing on the stage but just genuinely with your heart, helping the people who really need some help and support. So, I just want to say thank you so much. But to you, your guides, whoever comes along, including your angels as well, so thank you so much. Thank you for watching. And we'll see you on the next WHY's words episode.

Kay Thank you, Cheryl

"RISING FROM THE ASHES"

If anyone would like to connect with Kay, then you can do so by connecting with her directly at: *https://www.kayausterberry.co.uk*

See Kay sharing her WHYs Words at the Live
Love Laugh Live in October 2020 via this:
YouTube link: *https://youtu.be/b79eMzg6i8Q*

INTRODUCING AWARD WINNING INTERNATIONAL SPEAKER AND EVERYDAY INFLUENCER

Francesca Keating

As an Everyday Influencer, you can help others by sharing your experiences and Francesca Keating did just that When I first met Francesca I was stuck by her mane of red hair and an Irish passion to go with it.

Francesca has a wealth of knowledge and that can sometimes be a problem, how much do you share with the audience, without them becoming overwhelmed or feeling like they have all the information to try to achieve results without you?

If you've ever been told "I need to think about it"

Then it may be that you have filled your audience's head (potential clients) with too much and they literally need to go away and think about what you have shared.

This is ok if you are a teacher sharing just wisdom. However, if you know that the knowledge alone won't help them and that they need you to help implement the information, then it would be a dis-service.

Why? Because, if someone goes away to "think about it" and life gets busy, they could forget how much they really need you and your service.

With Francesca, I wanted her to share something that meant a lot to her and after a lifetime in nursing, caring for others was a way of life.

Here is the interview I did recently with Francesca if you would like to see where her focus is now in her 70's.

If you prefer to watch the video, please use this link:

https://youtu.be/A0OLNzq8tro

Cheryl Hello and welcome to WHY's Words, where I'm speaking to amazing women who are sharing their wisdom, their outlook on life, and the lessons that they've learned to be able to help other people like you. Today I am welcoming such an amazing, incredible soul. I met Francesca, six or seven years ago. You know, when someone comes into your life and then goes out again and comes back again and again and again, and every time I meet, I'm just so amazed by what she's doing and where she is. I've already introduced her; this lovely lady is called Francesca.
You've done amazing things in your life. Every time I speak to you, there's a story. But I want to just ask you about now, and what it is that you are focusing on right now, particularly in the next few weeks.

Francesca Going back to fix some things. I started pre-COVID and now I want to go back, see how they're up to see what's happening. And that involves going to Africa.

Cheryl Fabulous. And whereabouts in Africa are you going to be going?

Francesca We are going to Mozambique, which is in Sub-Saharan Africa. It's in northern Mozambique, Niassa. And to get to it, there's no direct route that's a bit torturous. So, we get to see Kenya, get to see Ethiopia, and then we come over into Malawi by road.

Cheryl Amazing. And you said that you've been there a few times before.

Francesca Yes. My first visit was back in 2003 when I came as the medical token person, with the vicar and a couple of other worthyies from the parish of St Mary's in Hampton. And they were looking to see what they could do if they partnered and trying to make the good folk of Hampton Parish a little bit more missionary and concept and outward looking.

Cheryl Very good. And you've been there. What role did you go in?

Francesca So, I just went along in case any of them got sick and carry the paracetamol. I did get accused of bringing an operating theatre.

Cheryl Is that not true or is that true?

Francesca Well, you never know. You've got to be prepared.

Cheryl Let me just clarify. I'm presuming you do have a medical background.

Francesca Yes, I'm a nurse.

I'm a mental health nurse. I'm on the Register of Nurses for England Wales. You'll find out more about that later. And I practised as a midwife, but I'm no longer a midwife because I couldn't. We must reregister every three years. And you've got to have had supervised practice. And I couldn't achieve all three and it seemed like too much.

Cheryl So, might sound like a silly question, but why Africa? Why Mozambique?

Francesca Well, that was where the wind blew me in. I hadn't chosen to go there. It seemed like a good idea. And I was at St Mary's University in Twickenham at the time, and I was trying to work up a stunning thesis to put in for my final year and I thought yeah! this will give me the material I want. It was theology and world religion, so it sort of fitted with a different culture and, and so I did, but then it took hold in lots of other ways. So, it was much more than that.

Cheryl So, you get there, you get to Africa, you're going out there, as you said, a bit of a mission, if you like, to do some good things. And then when you got there, what was it that kind of, as you said, grabbed hold of you.

Francesca That people could be so happy in abject poverty and misery with nothing? They were just so grateful to see us, they were so excited, they thought it was wonderful. They laid out spreads for us everywhere we went, and we found it was all the food they had, not just in the house, in the village. Um, and the men took the leading role in entertaining the guests. But I was kind of let loose. I wandered away from them and lived in what it was like in their little houses and the little congregations in which they were living, how hard it was just to get water and just to put a meal on the table. And I mean a meal, they didn't always put a meat on the table, but the meal they put on every evening was poor. And breakfast not so much. Didn't see any breakfasts, just one meal cooked in the evening.

Cheryl When I heard you talk recently, sharing a story about a young girl called Isanati?

Francesca Isanati yes.

Cheryl And she kind of really grabbed hold of a bit of a wave of help.

Francesca There were a lot of people like Isanati. but her story was just one that, you know, when something happens, you just turn around and you go oh f***. And you can't, your brain goes numb, and you can't think what has happened there. What could I do? I was powerless. Nobody was able to do anything. It just unfolded in front of us. And so, her story, I kind of thought it had to count for something. There had to be something that would become of It. I was witnessing that for a reason.

Cheryl And so, she was giving birth at the time.

Francesca She was giving birth. And I just tipped up at the health centre like I was doing every morning, see what was going down, see where it could help, and there she was lying there. And she couldn't push, she couldn't do anything, she couldn't help, the delivery baby was stuck. And yeah, the baby was born, lived for a short time and expired. And her mother came in and she'd lost five babies, she'd lost five! Three born just like this one and two, she'd had twins that had not lasted very long either, but they'd made it a few months, I think they made it into their first year.

Cheryl I remember thinking that even about the five children that she'd lost, it would be quite shocking. I'm sure you'd agree. But then she was. How old?

Francesca Fifteen.

Cheryl Wow, we've had many conversations haven't we, where people have said, what are the things that people ask you for?

And you say, well, they'll ask, you know, well, what's wrong with contraception? Why can't we solve that? And I know in your story you do tell a very funny part, which we'll not share now, if you want to see that, you must watch the video. But with regards to contraception, what's the problem? Like, now, why do people have a lot of children in Africa? Why is contraception not used?

Francesca Well, mostly the women on a replacement program. They have a child; they lose it, and they want another. Quite often, the partner doesn't survive more than two attempts. He goes on to somebody else and then she finally gets another partner. And she must have a child with them. That's the way It works.

Cheryl What happens with contraception?

Francesca Contraception. The men do not like it. It's against the culture. It's against everything. They get very, very irate, and indignant and come stamping their feet and threatening to beat up aid workers who dish out contraceptives, uh, condoms. Um, there were some that tried to implant the contraceptive in their arms and things, and that didn't go down well. Um, and pills. Pills don't work because you just can't get a regular supply, and it relies on a regular supply, so they can't secretly take the pill. But the condom is more important because it protects from other forms of venereal disease. So, with HIV rife there, it protects them a bit more.

Cheryl Yes. And I know when you share in the presentation that you were doing about how it's about educating and both learning about what to do best

Francesca Oh, yes. They taught me probably more than I taught them in the way that a culture evolves and the way that they internalise their beliefs and the way it becomes part of what they think and do and how it keeps them going. Their spirituality, you can't question, it's certainly there. And that's why they adapt so easily to things like Christianity and anything where there's a bit of prancing around and dressing up. You know me, sorry, God. But they take to that straight away because, oh, yes, we can see how this works.

Cheryl You're heading out there again as we are speaking now in August 2023, just in a few weeks. What is it that you want to do? You want to just review how things are like since you were there last?

Francesca Well, I think it's in a way, back to being the first time again and seeing what they have made of the last few years, how has COVID affected them. Um, I know that it has affected them in that there's been no tourism, there's been no visitors. Um, just as I couldn't go just as anybody else, um, but I don't know how they've survived themselves and what they have worked up from the things that we were practising and teaching them when we were there. What they've done with the ultrasound program, where is that up to and what do they need now to take any of these programs forward? How can we contribute to making that a reality and embedding it again?

Cheryl And you keep saying we. So, who's we? Who's going to Africa with you?

Francesca Well, there's a lovely lady who stood up and volunteered, and I love a volunteer. Didn't even have to put a shilling in a cup. So, Jane has decided that she would like to sample Africa. I know she'll love it. It gets hold of you.

Cheryl Yeah. Jane Leonard, who has played rugby for England. She was the captain of the combined services rugby team that was in the army for about ten years. I remember listening to a conversation that you were talking about uh what shall we say…toilets and toilet habits, Jane looked horrified. I remember you just said you've been in the army, haven't you? Which is quite funny, but you're going to go out there and Jane is going to be playing sports with the children.

Francesca Yes, we've already been in touch with some of the education team out there that we were working with before, and they're very excited. They have bought schools now, so they're very excited to go and everyone's keen to get ladies rugby going or girls' rugby. And so, Jane's working that up. They've got five schools on the list at the moment. There probably will be more. So, she's going to go and trip up there and show them how it's done, and they will show her what they know. But I think football is vicious and rugby has more contact. We'll see. We'll see.

Cheryl I think she was talking about putting tags on, so they don't have to go in and tackle, you know, break bones and things like that. They're going to do it in a very health and safety way, shall we say for those that are playing.

Francesca I'm nodding wisely and thinking maybe a larger first aid kit than last time.

Cheryl And now all of this is not being funded by anybody else. This is you and Jane giving up your time going out there. And so, you were asking in a Bob Geldof style way.

Francesca Giving us ya f****** money.

Cheryl Just because obviously this is something that's close to your heart. You're sharing this, you know, with Jane. Jane is going to be sharing it on social media to bring awareness with it, because I know a lot of people would say, well, why don't you help people closer to home? Why Africa? What would you say to that?

Francesca Why Africa? Why anywhere? It's a one world. we're not all divided into little silos. Covid did a great job of putting us back into little silos. Let's break free again. What we are doing here. Climate change in the Western world is affecting them more than us now. This is the second summer. Wow. They've had floods, cyclones, and drought. All their seasonal variations in weather are totally on its head, not just through Africa, through India. The oceans are getting warmer. You know, we need to help them to reach a generation that's going to fix this because we've certainly messed it up. It's all our problem. It's not just a few people living in their village there, but it must start somewhere.

Cheryl And it's interesting because if you look on YouTube, you'll see on Instagram, you know, lots of lovely videos of the children, you know, dancing and having a great time. And we kind of talked about this didn't we.

Francesca Yeah, well, they do. Yeah, they do. they'll get up and dance for anything. You just hold your mobile phone up with the tune on and they're away.

Cheryl It's good to see, isn't it.

Francesca It is good to see. But they take adversity in their stride because that's all they've known.

Cheryl Yeah. So, what we say is, if you really like watching these videos of the kids, you know, dancing, does it put a smile on your face? Of course, it does. Because you want children to be happy regardless of whether you know that child. And so that's why, £5, for example, what can you do with £5 in Africa?

Francesca £5, 125 doses of pain relief. That's to start. Even something like that is hard to get there.

Cheryl £60 a year.

Francesca £60 a year will send a child to school with a uniform and some books. So, he looks the same as his peers. Even if he's clever enough to get into the school, he won't be able to go and he won't go without the uniform. They must conform, they must look the same, and that's very important to them to give them a little bit of status.

Cheryl And later down in the line, you talk about maybe sponsoring children. and people being in touch with them.

Francesca And yes.

Cheryl In touch with, in particular some of the brighter children who were sponsored and then someone made a pledge to continue sponsoring them and so that they went on to higher education and had more opportunities to bring that learning back to the village and bring that learning back to school. Some of them became the teachers who are now in the new primary schools.

Cheryl And so, Francesca, what do people need to do if they want to contribute and donate and help you and Jane on this journey of discovery.

Francesca Well, on this trip we're looking at Go Fund Me. So, we've got a Go Fund Me page. There is a link to it, go there and yeah, take it from there. Link up with us. We are two women that are here to change things and change is what needs to happen. Yeah, we're motivated, we want to do it and we want to help other women, to help their children to grow into the world that we'd like to see.

Cheryl We'll pop it underneath this video. Francesca is 70 (Mmmm) years old plus won't say it exactly.

Francesca You can go off people.

Cheryl And it would be easy for you to just stay home with your dog and watch the telly and continue to do the work that you do and not do this. And so, I think it's only fair that if you want to make a difference, even, you know, just £5. You know what £5 can buy you in this day and age, probably a coffee and maybe a cake. If you're lucky, if you'd be willing to contribute that towards, you know, somebody that you don't know yet, but that would make a difference in the life then I'm sure you'd join me in wishing Francesca and Jane all the best on their trip. And Francesca, thank you so much for just being incredible, amazing and giving sometimes to your own detriment. I know this but thank you for being you. You are amazing. And I'll give you some of my f****** money.

Francesca Thank you so.

Cheryl Thank you so much for watching. And remember to keep standing up and speaking out and just sharing your wisdom like Francesca has here. We'll see you soon on the next episode

See Francesca sharing her WHYs Words
https://youtu.be/ohybE7BaBB4?

CHAPTER 6

The Successful Solution Framework™

To have the right PRODUCT, in other words how to decide what you want to share with your audience, there are 3 main areas to choose from.

I developed **The Successful Solution Framework™** to guide my clients to include 1 or all 3 of these in their capacity as Freedom Speakers and Everyday Influencers.

Your PRODUCT is what you have as a service or experience that you know can help others.

You can turn this wisdom into a product.

Let's see which one (or all) are relevant for you. To make it easy, they all begin with P!

Personal

You may already know that you want to help people on a personal level because you've trained in this area and now you have a proven way to guide others, e.g. with life coaching. This may be where you have gained qualifications to share the systems you learned to help others.

Maybe you haven't done any courses yet but I would say maybe your personal experience is how you can help others. Famously, Tony Robbins, these days regarded as a celebrity in the industry, at the start of his journey when others asked what his qualifications were, simply replied: "I have a qualification in results!"

Look at yourself, as discussed previously, maybe you've already been your own first client. Look at what you did to get yourself to a better place. Look at the steps you took, take out the ones that didn't work and focus on the ones that did. Guess what? Now you are able to see what the strategy is that you followed. Would you agree that if you could find someone with a similar problem that you'd be able to help them too?

Yes, it would be good to have some techniques (tools in the toolkit so to speak) that are proven strategies. These are to ensure you do no harm to others, but they do not necessarily mean you have to study for years. As an Everyday Influencer, you are able to support everyday people with everyday problems and this of course means there is every day too. Now is when they are needed - not when you believe you have enough certificates.

I remember when Marion and myself started the Find Your WHY foundation. I wanted to study – I did life coaching, NLP, Human Design training and then there was the speaker training and business growth development. Interestingly, during the first session we held, I used none of these skills. Marion used her skills (from her time in India) and I used the skills I had already used in business. Looking back, we could have started a year earlier and helped hundreds of people in that year, instead of me waiting to be perfect!

If you haven't got certificates, it doesn't mean to say you can't help others while you learn. Make a list of all the personal challenges you have overcome that you know others could benefit from or indeed have benefited from.

Write down what you did to help them.

Did you give them some advice?

What was that advice?

I know you may think it was nothing, it was everything – it helped them feel better, right? And who else did you help? Here you start to understand that you already know enough. Stop waiting to be perfect and start to help those who need some help. Interestingly, you can learn as you go and guess what? Your earliest clients help you to understand what you still I need to learn. If you don't know the answers, say "I have never come across that before, let me check it out and get back to you." Then make sure you do. Next time that situation comes along, bingo, you have the answer.

If you look Izabella Niewiadomska up on the internet you will find several articles sharing how she transformed her unhealthy lifestyle, stress, and illness to a healthier one where she has been called a "Super-Ager" reducing her metabolic age and her appearance by a decade. Izabella now helps other women to achieve the same. Izabella is an everyday Influencer. Take a read or watch on video the interview I did with her in July 2023.

If you prefer to watch the video, please use this link:
https://youtu.be/cQ_BObNpDrE

INTRODUCING AWARD WINNING
SPEAKER AND EVERYDAY INFLUENCER

Izabella Niewiadomsk

Cheryl Today I'm joined by an incredible soul. I feel like I want to say "dzień dobry" (good day). This lovely lady is from Poland, and I've known her for a few years now. In fact, we met speaking at a university and then we went on to become Association of Transformational Leader members with the amazing Marie Diamond. And so, this lovely lady, please introduce yourself.

Izabella Well, yes, sometimes they call me Izabella with an unpronounceable surname. My name is Izabella Niewiadomska, and I'm a wellness and mindset coach and a health strategist. I'm also a bestselling author and transformational leader, you can go on and on, there are so many on the list. But my passion is really working with people and making a positive difference in their lives to become Association of Transformational Leader members with the amazing Marie Diamond.

Cheryl Well, I always remember Izabella from when I first met her, and she always had this amazing red lipstick, you know when you look at someone, you just go, how come they just look so amazing every time you see them?

Izabella Well, red is my colour. Looks like yours too today!

Cheryl Today we're red-Ing together. Yeah. So, Izabella, I know I saw you recently standing on stage, and you were sharing your journey, which is incredible. The bit that I love, and I love all of it, but I want to really address straight away is the bit that you were talking about at the end, where quite recently you were chatting away. It was some Chinese ladies that were in a room, and you said to them how old you were, and they were like, what?! Do you want to share that story with us?

Izabella Yeah, It was funny, it was not just one occasion. Recently a lot of people were kind of surprised at my age. At a recent book launch of my friend, there were ladies who were watching me, and in fact, they came to compliment my dress. And when we started chatting they asked me, so, you know, what do you do to look so well? And I said, well, I'm 60, and they said, What? They couldn't believe it. And they said, you know, we want everything that you did, what do you do? Obviously, it's very flattering when people compliment you, and what can I say? It's down to lifestyle and lifestyle choices. I'm not sure if it's in my genes, although my parents do look younger too than their age. But I think that a lot of it, how we look, has to do with how we look after ourselves.

Cheryl And you've been in several magazines and Daily Mail a few years ago.

Izabella Well, yes, that's what happened. I think it was 2011 when I wanted to expand my business. I started to go to networking events and people noticed the way I looked, noticed my energy, and suddenly I was invited to be interviewed by Daily Mail, by Top Centre, by Women Fitness and many other different magazines and publications. And I was also on different shows, podcasts, and Sky TV, and they all wanted to know what did I do. The reality is that everybody wants to have more energy.

Everybody wants to look good and feel good. And somehow the word 'delicious' became my word, and to me everything is delicious, and I just love to bask in the deliciousness of life. But yes, when you live your truth, when you are authentic, when you do what you love, it comes across. Bottom line, I didn't look for any publicity, didn't search for any PR. They found me. People simply recommended me to newspapers, to magazines so, there I was. The Daily Mail called me a 'Super Ager'.

Izabella aged 43

Izabella aged 53

Cheryl I love that! Super Ager!

Izabella Yes, new title

Cheryl Fabulous. But if we go back, I mean, obviously this is where you are now. But there was a time, when you were much younger, where you were eating the right things and you were being physically active, etc., but there was still a problem. What was that, that you had?

Izabella Well, it was in 1986. I was 23 and one day I ended up in the hospital temporarily paralysed with loss of speech. I was in another country at a cultural conference and then one morning I woke up on a hospital bed. I had no clue how

I got in there and it was a very unnerving experience. I thought I nearly died. And so, I looked at my life and tried to analyze what was it that I was doing, that it was not right, because like you said, I felt I was doing all the right things. Well, I admit, I was a bit naughty because I used to smoke and drink socially, mostly at the parties so, clearly, I wasn't a saint. But when I looked back, I understood that I clearly underestimated the impact of stress on my body, on my health and wellbeing.

The thing is, people tell us - work hard, hard work is recognised and rewarded, push yourself outside your comfort zone, etc. But people don't really tell you or teach you what to do to replenish yourself, what to do and how often you need to recharge your batteries, and so you push yourself harder and harder. And eventually you burn out. It's a lot like a rubber band - you stretch it, and then you stretch a bit more and more and then it snaps. Then you realise, okay, something must change. And I love Jim Rohn, who was my mentor for many years said: "For things to change, you've got to change, for things to get better you've got to get better". I love this quote because it means, hey, you are in charge and you can take charge of your life, you can take control and if you change, things will change and things will get better, but it starts with you. So, I took that on board, and I went on a quest to study and research, to find out what really impacts health, and what to do to be healthy, to be well and to feel good. What I've learned and discovered transformed my life. I feel fabulous. When I turned 60, my metabolic age was 26! So, when people ask me, how old are you, I'm translating that in my head into "How young are you"? And I'm amused thinking, should I say 26 or 60? That's just a bit of fun.

Cheryl So, you did work out that there are like four main elements, I think you said, you found out that there was a secret, didn't you?

Izabella Yes, there is. I realised that there are four areas, four habits that have a profound impact on our health, well-being, on our energy, performance and on the way we look and feel. In fact, they impact all areas of our life. And the first area is related to what we eat, to our eating habits. Food has a huge impact on our physiology, psychology, and emotional wellbeing, on how we look, feel and perform each day. The second area relates to our movement, to how much we exercise, to our fitness habits. We've got to move, there's no question about it. it's just so important. The third area explores our engagement, our interactions with people, our communication habits. They have a huge impact on our career, on our social life, on the quality of our personal and professional relationships and on our overall health and wellbeing. And then there is the fourth area that relates to how we handle our emotions, how we respond to stress, to stressful situations, how we behave when we are challenged, when we are under pressure. I mean, I don't know about you, but I think that stress is a part of our life. In fact, medical research says that 90% of all our illnesses and diseases are related to stress. We can't control stress but what we can control is how we respond to stress and how we control our emotions. That's practical wisdom or Inner Peace Habits. And then I looked at those four areas and I realised that there is still something missing, a little secret that without it all those four areas are not going to work well. That secret is explained in what I call the Practical P.A.C.E. Method, that I developed. Where P.A.C.E represents a method that helps you to recognise priorities, to implement and take control of all those four areas that I've just talks about. To harness and master them, to replenish yourself effectively and instantly transform the quality of your life with renewed energy and clear mental focus. Because let's face it, when you are overwhelmed, physically tired and mentally exhausted, you cannot do much. Often when you are tired you can't think straight, you don't feel like doing anything, sometimes you don't even want to play with your children. So, if you want to be healthy, look younger, perform better, recover quicker, if you want to have vitality, live for 120 years then clearly, you need to master this journey of health and wellness. You need to learn to P.A.C.E. yourself, to replenish effectively, to master your energy levels or otherwise you may fall into a trap, just like I did when I was 23. I mean, I've been working in the health and well-being and personal development industry for the last 31 years right now, and over the years I've seen people with great hearts who have so much to give. Many great leaders, entrepreneurs, mothers, fathers, and I've seen that many of them followed some of the habitual patterns that took me to a hospital bed. And I know that if they just followed the Practical P.A.C.E. Method that I developed, they would be able to avoid it. Also they would be able to unleash their full potential, to align with their essence, with their deliciousness, share their gifts, to live a life of fulfilment.

Cheryl Yeah, I know you spoke about that, and if anyone wants to find out more, then we'll put the link below to the talk that you did. It is a great example of how you took your knowledge and turned it into a training product to sit with your physical health and nutrition products.

Just in closing, I know that you talked about being able to change your mindset around. And it's interesting, you talk about pace because you had in your mind a few years ago that you would never do running and you didn't want to do running, what happened there then?

Izabella Well, all my life I believed that I cannot run and then when I turned 50, I think something changed in me. Maybe I just saw some friends picking up running at the later stage of their lives. And I just felt, why not me? Why not try at least, why not give it a go? And I was just fortunate to come across a program called *5 weeks to 5K*, prepared by a famous Olympic medalist from Sydney Olympics, a sprinter. I just thought okay let's follow it. So, I just started, couldn't fit it at all into my daily schedule at the start, not until I got the emotional connection with my reason why I wanted to do it. And then I did 5K. I felt exhilarated. And then I thought, okay, why not 10K? When I did 10K, I thought, why not 25 and maybe 50? Sounds cool, especially as I just had turned 50 not long before that. And then two and a half years later I completed a 100K ultra run, which is like two and a half marathons.

Cheryl Fabulous! Is this in one go?

Izabella Yes, in one go, 100 kilometres in one go and I completed that. What was crucial was that I recovered in 24 hours without any muscle pain whatsoever. And that was for me the proof that the Practical P.A.C.E. Method that I developed works even in circumstances like that.

Cheryl Amazing!

Izabella Because you've got to pace yourself. You cannot just run 100 kilometres without pacing yourself. It's impossible. So, pacing and my P.A.C.E. method applies to every area of our life. You want to pace yourself in your business, in your relationships, in everything that you do, and prioritise your commitments. Everything is about P.A.C.E.

Cheryl Brilliant! and if people would love to find out more about how they can pace themselves so that they can be 28, or look 28 when they're 60, where can they connect with you?

Izabella Well, I love immediate interaction with people. I like to talk to people. So below this video, you'll find my telephone number, message me. Then we can book a call and we can just go from there.

Cheryl Thank you. Thank you so much for joining us. As I said, if you'd like to connect with Izabella to find out how you can be deliciously you, pinching your word, then the number will be below this video. Thank you so much, Izabella "dziękuję" (thank you) for being here.

Izabella Perfect! Yes, thank you.

Cheryl I will say goodbye, and we look forward to seeing you in the next video when we speak to more WHY's women sharing their wisdom with you. In the meantime, remember to keep standing up and speaking out. See you soon.

To find out more about Izabella or to connect with her, you can do so at:
Telephone: +44 7968 953149
LinkedIn: *https://uk.linkedin.com/in/izabellaniewiadomska*
Facebook: *https://www.facebook.com/izabella.niewiadomska.7*
Instagram: *https://www.instagram.com/nutritiousmi*

Professional

Maybe you would prefer to help others in their profession and so here you have experience in a particular industry, or you have experienced some pain, which you have overcome.

As with the **Personal** aspect above, I have experienced the same limiting beliefs from many clients. However, here the big belief for many is that the solution they have for their client can only be done on a 1:1 basis (this does come up for personal too, just more so here). This means that they can only help a limited number of people, mainly because there are only 24 hours a day and only one of you!

I learned from Andy Harrington the power of working one to many and how to leverage your knowledge. In the last 8 years, I have helped thousands of entrepreneurs to be able to put their business knowledge into a framework that can be turned into an information product, for example an online video teaching program, and can be shared to many others at the same time, all while you don't need to be there physically. Think about that for the moment, this is where the 'making money while you sleep' can become a reality!

When was the last time you shared some information that you had already shared with someone else that day, week or month? The truth is there are only so many problems in business and therefore only so many solutions required. Your solutions are the unique way you help your clients and instead of you saying the same thing over and over to a different audience, there are elements of your business that can be delivered this way, leaving you with more time to work 1:1 on the issues that you can ask for a higher investment on. This means that the more someone gets of your time, the higher the investment. I liken this to cooking. There are multiple options. You can go out and get all the shopping yourself and make a meal, which takes time and energy. You can go and get a takeaway and spend less time and energy to get the food. You can go to a restaurant and now you don't even need to wash up. Or you could get a personal chef to come in and cook for you and do all the cleaning up too. In each case you eat, right?

However, the investment goes up depending on the service you get and the more hands off or bespoke the service is. The same is true in your business. The more you do for your client, the more reward you get in the way of money.

This leads me nicely into another potential limiting belief and this is one I hear all the time. "I don't know if people will pay for my services" or the classic "I don't know how much to charge." You can of course look at your competitors and charge a little less to be competitive, but please don't do this. People will potentially come to you because you are the cheapest and in my humble experience you will potentially end up working all hours, just to make ends meet.

Or you can be the most expensive in the industry -I've heard "add a zero to the price you think." Love the logic in that ...NOT!

Here are my suggestions:

Make a list of all the training you've done and add up all the investment you have made here too using this formula:

Cost of the actual training + additional costs (travel/hotel) + (hours of your time to complete × your average hourly rate) + cost of materials (books, tools, certificates)

For example, when I trained with Marisa Peer to become an Advanced Rapid Transformational Therapist and Clinical Hypnotherapist the total investment was just under £50,000. In case you think, "that's OK for you Cheryl, I don't have that amount", neither did I.

I borrowed and begged to do this I invested in a big way.

The reason why this is an important step is that when it comes to asking others to pay to benefit from the skills you have invested in, this puts it into perspective. And here's the sad truth - many new entrepreneurs and especially enlightened souls don't add in their time to the cost which is a FUNDAMENTALLY FLAWED approach.

Miss this out and you're not valuing yourself and here's the thing if you don't value you, how can you expect anyone else to?

This 'cost exercise' is something I learned in my manufacturing background. The raw materials are added in, the cost of the factory, design cost and the people on the payroll got paid, so why would you not pay yourself as an entrepreneur?

Knowing that I invested over £50,000 in learning this technique means that I do not hesitate when I quote my clients. I know I can help them to invest in themselves too. I can help someone overcome a block or barrier in their life in 2 hours and my clients say this is priceless because they get their lives back. In this case they are paying for my knowledge, experience and the investment I made with Marisa

Not for the 2 hours, does that make sense? I recouped the £50,000 investment with clients within 1 year and helped 50 clients with personal breakthroughs. This was just one investment I made. Adding in all the other development courses I did, (books, online training, etc) I'd say that it is closer to £250,000 in a 3-year period. What can I say? My clients get real value.

How much have you invested in your development?

A lot of people look at the price of moving forward rather than the cost of standing still. Another way to look at the price of working with you is based on your experience. In other words, if you've been your first client, as previously mentioned, what would you have paid to avoid the pain you had to go through back in the day that you had to invest your time (there it is again) and the knocks you took to figure out? Here you will find the price you paid - put a value on what you would have invested to avoid all that pain.

Irrespective of the investment you made to learn a technique (or a modality as often used in personal development) or the strategy you used to get yourself away from a painful situation, you had a strategy and it is this that others can benefit from usually in a much shorter time period! As the saying goes, time is money!

If you don't have a product or service just yet and you do want one, there is 1 thing that I can share with you straight away. It is possible for you to already have enough information and life experiences to help others and when you have a framework to show the tangible ways others can follow your solutions, this is now an asset - something to make you an income.

When I first met Susanna Reay, it was at an event in London run by Nick James. I was sharing a stage with Steven Bartlett and Marie Forelo. The day was long with 12 speakers before me. Honestly, some were excellent and inspirational and so not so good in terms of speaker skills, which meant that their presentations were coming across as boring.

Nick had come over to say "Cheryl you're a professional speaker – please lift the energy in the room"

On I go and in my usual way, I wake the crowd up.

Interestingly, after my presentation, which at the time was all about Finding Your Why, your purpose in your professional and personal lives.

Nick said "If I hear your name one more time, I'm going to scream"

He clearly saw the confusion on my face "We are going round asking who was the best speaker of the day and all we keep hearing is Cheryl Chapman"

It was the way I delivered the presentation that was getting the most attention. And so that is when I realised, I needed to help entrepreneurs to be more engaging. It was apparent they knew how to educate but very few knew how to entertain. Suzanna had a wealth of knowledge and her presentations were far from dull, she had mastered the art of a colourful and organised framework. In fact, she was helping others to do the same.

Her organic marketing was gaining traction, however, the inspiration and instant income generator from a presentation to a few hundred people had eluded her because she is an introvert. However, she knew she had an amazing product to help others.

INTRODUCING AWARD WINNING SPEAKER AND EVERYDAY INFLUENCER

Susanna Reay

Susanna Reay is an award-winning business coach, speaker and author specialising in frameworks. Bringing visual clarity to her clients, enabling her clients to scale their business with ease.

Here is the interview I did recently with Susanna at The Confidently Come Speaking Event in July 2023. If you prefer to watch the video, please use this link: *https://youtu.be/sywffiClwGQ*

Cheryl Hi, and welcome to WHY's Words with Why's women here at the Strictly Speaking events. Today I'm joined by an amazing, incredible woman. I met this woman about six months ago. And, you know, when you just see somebody and you're like, this person just means business and she knows her business. And then once she started speaking, I was like, oh, yes, we need to invite her to our stage because people need to know about her. So, you might be thinking, who is this? So, I'm going to hand it over, please introduce yourself.

Susanna My name is Susanna Reay and I'm an Online Business Mentor, and I like to say I'm the Chief Spark at The Spark Space because I love sparking ideas in people.

Cheryl Love it, love it, love it. Of course, we'll be sharing a bit more about Spark's ideas. So, I remember seeing you on stage quite recently, and if I remember rightly, you started out with six thousand and I was like, oh my gosh, I heard that you travelled a lot, and I wondered if these were the countries that you've been to. But tell the viewers what six thousand is about.

Susanna Not quite the number of countries I've been to, but six thousand is the number of thoughts that we have in a day, and that's a lot of thoughts. So, some of these are just thoughts that are like moving your hands around but some of these thoughts will be ideas that we can use and implement in our business. So hence the start of the talk.

Cheryl Nice, I loved it, I loved it- and before you had your own business, what was your background? What was it when you realised that you could, you know, be creative and have these ideas. Where did that all start?

Susanna Oh gosh, realistically, I've been having ideas ever since I was a child. I've been creative right from the get-go. My first degree was in Art and Design, and then I went on and did an MBA at Business School because I realised, I'm at this intersection between business and design. And it was when I was talking to friends in the bar, and they might be running a business and they would go; 'Oh, Susanna, what do you think about this?' And I'd naturally be solving their issues for them just over a drink. And it was then that they turned around to me and said, 'Susanna, you should totally do this as a business!' And I guess that is how it started out in terms of being on the consultancy coaching side because, as you inferred, that I have lived across three continents, five countries, and twenty cities in my lifetime. And so, I've grown up with the Internet and working online, and therefore it became a natural extension to help people promote their business online because that was how I was connecting with all my network, basically.

Cheryl Amazing and I know that you started to create an alternative way because when you were going to network meetings or when you were with other people, there was this kind of very gregarious in-your-face method, and you give yourself the label of introvert. Now I've got to say I'm an introvert. Until I met you and had this kind of explanation, I used to think it was the wallflower in the corner facing the wall. So, do you want to share with other people who might not be in the know like I am now?

Susanna Yeah. Not at all, being introverted is about how you harness your energies. So, if you like to gather your energies more on your own, then you are more introverted in nature. Whereas if you're an extrovert, you love being around other people and you gain energy from being around other people. So, you can be a sociable introvert, or you could be a shy introvert like the wallflower.

But there's eight different types of introverts in Confidently Come Speaking the same way there's eight different types of extroverts. The traditional marketing networking is very extrovert-friendly, shall I say, because it's about going out, meeting lots of people, and talking about yourself and I just found that exhausting. I would go into a venue, and it might only be an hour, and I couldn't work for the rest of the day because I was so drained. Whereas if I have a one-to-one conversation with someone, that will energise me because it would be sparking ideas and thoughts and you'd be generating like having a deeper conversation. And so yeah, it's about how you energise yourself. And yeah, I totally had to rewrite that extrovert-biased marketing rule book and find a way that suited myself.

Cheryl So, you wrote your own book, is that correct?

Susanna I did yes.

Cheryl Do you have It here?

Susanna I have it here, it's 'The Introvert Way® Roadmap' and I've trademarked The Introvert Way® in fact. It's the roadmap that I discovered and followed over the time thatI was basically working and trying to fathom it out for myself. I was also working with more and more introverted entrepreneurs, because this was pre-pandemic. So, it was before the rest of the world had come online. I was introverted already, as I called it, on the dark side and happily playing in that space. And so, I'd had 20 years' experience of what works, what doesn't work and I realised, thanks to my clients, really. I was running a mastermind and it got to a point where they were going; 'Yes but how do you do it, Susanna? Because I'm so exhausted too.' And I realised I hadn't been sharing the framework that I'd built my whole business upon, and so that's kind of how the book came about.

I always say it was years in the making in my head, but it only took six weeks to write because it had been years in the making. So, I think sometimes you just know when a book is ready to be birthed and you don't want to push and try and write something just for the sake of writing a book, you've got to wait until you've got a genuine message to share.

Cheryl I love it. I love a couple of things here. One is that 'use your introverted superpowers'. So obviously that's coming from an introvert with superpowers. We love this and I love your analogy there, if you're pregnant, not that I've ever been pregnant, but you have, and if you've ever been pregnant, you don't start pushing after month three, you know, you wait until it's ready. So, I love that analogy, a great book. I also know just in terms of colours and designs, what I really love about a book and the framework information that you have is that you can take complex ideas and make them very simple for people to understand, even though they've got depth and layers underneath, which is amazing.

Susanna Yeah, because the joy is when you simplify something down to a core concept and make it understandable, it then becomes repeatable and most importantly shareable. Because a lot of us as well, if you're a coach or a consultant, you're in the business of transformation and therefore you want to share your ideas on how you are helping people transform. Because you're helping others get better basically, and so you want to share your methods. The simpler we can make that and the easier it is for everyone to understand, the better really, it's just a win-win all around.

Cheryl Yeah, and so you mentioned coaches and consultants. Who else have you worked with? I know you've had quite a breadth, but just sort of maybe three or four to share with us.

Susanna Energy workers, designers, driving instructors, accountants, everything both left and right brain. Because the joy about frameworks is it works for everyone and it doesn't really matter where you come from, whether it's the holistic well-being space where I do work with quite a lot of people because they struggle the most in terms of sharing their value. Whereas even though I've had a huge impact with accountants as well, they have a title that people kind of presume they know what an accountant does, but there's also issues, even with accountants; people not really understanding what their speciality might be. So yeah, whether it's left or right brain, it can work for everyone. It's just about making it simple, understandable, and shareable, particularly now, where we've got such short attention spans, that you've got to capture people fast.

Cheryl Yeah, and that's why a lot of your frameworks are very colourful. They've got shapes, they've got like an easy flow to them. So, when you first look at it, it might only have three or four words on it, but again, it goes back to the depth that your clients have around the subject, isn't it?

Susanna Yeah, and they're designed for people, is not just to be shown flat, they're designed to be interactive. You present different elements at different times; if you base something on a simple Venn diagram, you talk about what's happening at the intersections, and then there's all the elements, (as the expert), that you know come together to make that impact. Because what we don't want to do when we're first talking to clients is to overwhelm them and confuse them with the how we want to focus on the impact on the result.

Cheryl Yeah, nice, and I know you've had a lot of success with your clients. Can you just share maybe one example of where somebody was and then what happened with them after that worked with you?

Susanna Yeah, I had one client and she's a voice energy healer, so a very specific area. And she was really struggling with even selling a basic $49 offer. When we dug down and worked in and discovered her framework, which for her was a spiral and she'd always had this feeling of it being a spiral because of it. From the inside and coming out. And in the spiritual sense, that is so self-actualisation, but she struggled to share this with her clients. So, we created a framework, and after creating that framework, she launched her online course and had 20K sales from that first launch. And she was totally blown away with the difference that the framework had. And that was because it really helped her clients see the immense value she gave, and she stopped overwhelming people.

She would talk for half an hour trying to explain what it was she did, and now she had a simple way to take people into her world, and they'd go, "Yeah, yeah, where do I sign up?" And it was huge difference.

Cheryl Brilliant! So, if there's anybody out there who's got a similar frustration, maybe they can talk very freely about what they do, but people are like, oh yes, thank you very much for that and then walking away. How can they get in touch with you so that they can benefit from this too?

Susanna So, the best way is for you to find me across all socials. My favourite is Instagram and LinkedIn, and that's @SusannaReay or via my website, which is SusannaReay.com.

Cheryl We'll also pop the links underneath this video. I hope that you've enjoyed listening to Susanna and it's sparked an idea for you and to connect with her so that she can help you grow your business as well.

Susanna, thank you so much. It sounds a little bit cliche but thank you so much for lighting up the entrepreneurial space for both extroverts and introverts.

Susanna Yeah, absolutely.

Cheryl Because of course, we will work with extroverts as well, because they do need frameworks too.

Susanna Extroverts can also struggle with talking too much, is all I'll say!

Cheryl Hmm I wonder who she's talking about there! And on that note, we will say thank you so much. Remember to stand up and keep speaking out and we'll see you in the next episode. Thank you, Susanna.

Susanna Thank you.

If you would like to connect with Susanna and find out more, you can do so here.
Website: *www.susannareay.com*
LinkedIn: *https://www.linkedin.com/in/susannareay*
Instagram: *https://www.instagram.com/susannareay*
Threads: *https://www.threads.net/@susannareay*
Facebook Page: *https://www.facebook.com/susannareaybusiness*

See Susanna sharing her words of wisdom at The Confidently Come Speaking Live in July 2023 via this

YouTube link: *https://youtu.be/I1YnXAtSq2U*

As well as wealth in business, there is also health and that is vitally important. After all, you wouldn't want to be the richest person in the graveyard, right?

The next speaker I'd like to introduce you to is a very busy professional whose focus is to guide others to better health with the use of some of her 4 legged friends.

INTRODUCING INTERNATIONAL AWARD WINNING SPEAKER

Wendy Firmin-Price

Wendy Firmin-Price is an Equine Assisted Therapist and Owner of The HEART Centre in Woking.
https://youtu.be/gnIMAoexSjU

Cheryl Now, OMG, have I got an amazing guest for you? This lady is full of heart, you'll know exactly what I mean about that in a moment. Her approach to life is slightly different, shall we say, from the average coach. And she's just one of the most amazing, heartfelt humans that I've ever met. So please, would you introduce yourself?

Wendy Aww, thank you, Cheryl. My name is Wendy Firmin-Price, and I run the Heart Equine Assisted Therapy and Coaching Center in Surrey. That's alongside The Holistic Horse & Pony riding centre and Healing Hearts and Minds with Horses Community Interest Company.

Cheryl Wow and so, when you say, like, therapy and horses, it's not kind of what you would normally just put together, like, you know, cream and an ice or ice and cream. So how do horses help in therapy?

Wendy Whether you are doing coaching or therapy, horses have a way to really help to act as a bit of a mirror and/or a metaphor for what's going on within you. Most of us know the belief systems that we have internally, but we don't realise how much they can leak out externally in our energy field. And so, because horses can read energy very, very well (after all that's what their whole life is about) as prey animals, they're able to read our energy field easily.

What some of us don't realise is that these patterns, beliefs, and emotional vibrations that leak out from our body influences the type of people that we attract into our lives, the situations we find ourselves in, and bring about all sorts of consequences. Therefore, when you are working with the horses, you can get accurate and immediate feedback. A classic example I can give you was the time when one of my clients came to me, wanting to develop her relationship with men but she always kept finding the wrong man and so is often the case, when we took her around to choose a horse, she got totally drawn to the horses that were unavailable (5 in total). Now, those horses might have been unavailable that day because they were being ridden later, or they belonged to someone else or the horse was lame or there was some circumstance making the horses unavailable! But you see that was the pattern of her belief system and energy field showing up, she had a vibration of always attracting and being attracted to unavailability. The horses instantly showed her what she had only talked about in years of therapy, another common situation that shows up instantly is how well you do or don't set boundaries. Within 10 minutes of handling the horses, how you start to hold the horses, demonstrates how you are with people straight away. The horses reveal whether you are clear in your decisions, they will show up, whether you set clear boundaries and mean it, on other words say what you mean, and mean what you say. I am regularly asked "Is the horse not responding because they're looking to make a problem or be cheeky or naughty?" but the answer is no because they are just responding to the energy field that is being given out. A common reaction when they sort of push you around, I normally hear "Oh I don't want to hurt them". Naturally, nor do I want you to hurt my horse! But all that's happening is you are being immediately shown all the patterns and beliefs that you don't realise is leaking out of you! Therefore, people are not respecting you, taking advantage and/or pushing you around. Once you find the belief system or the event that has created that coping strategy, between you, me, and the horses we can find the best solution for you to heal and grow. Now here's what I absolutely love most about the coaching I do with the horses. The moment you find the new belief, pattern, or strategy the horse immediately knows if you are just paying lip service or whether you really are embodying the new! You can't get away saying what you think the coach wants to hear. The feedback may be brutally honest but saves YEARS of therapy or coaching and therefore money

Cheryl Like a little extra tool.

Wendy Yes, because it's very easy with normal coaching to say what you think the coach wants to hear, but when you're with the horse, you can't B.S them, or should I say horse S them. You get truth and authenticity and so it clears years and years of stuff that has been leaking out of you quickly therefore change can be quite instant. And although HEART equine-assisted coaching may require a little bit more investment initially, it works out far more economically because you don't have to spend years in therapy.

Cheryl That's it, isn't it? You know, therapy, let's say, you know, some people go out there and do therapy for, you know, £50 an hour, for example. But if they must do that for 52 weeks of a year compared to what they might come and get from you quicker. And, I think that, if you're stuck in this situation where this block has been there, normally we don't go for help straight away. So, you might have been dealing with this for years, you know, and so, suddenly, I love the fact that it's kind of like an inside kind of job with the horse. It's like, yeah, no, no, no, that's not going to work. And how many horses do you have down at the centre?

Wendy We have nearly 30 horses, not all mine, just the bills and the hay and feed! This gives you a lovely variety to work with. We also vary how we do the sessions. We've got big fields where sometimes we do herd watching, or we may work in the stable, or we'll work in the arena leading or sometimes just being free with them.

Cheryl What happens if they say, "but I'm terrified of horses"?

Wendy I think that's perfect because that can show up something that we can really work on. From my experience, it can often reflect something to do with their power. It could be their feminine power, their masculine power or just standing in their power. And so, by coming and working with the horses we can get you to feel safe with your power. We've got 2 adorable little Shetland ponies here. They start everybody off if they're a bit nervous. But then usually because people just see such a shift in their energy so quickly, they're often working with the biggest horses by lunchtime.

Cheryl And so, if somebody is out there now, what kind of person could you help? What would they be going through, what's going on in their life right now?

Wendy So, the main sort of women (and increasing number of men) that come to me are entrepreneurs, businesswoman or mid-lifers that are very stressed, that are trying to juggle everything. They make time for everybody else and do everything for everyone else, but they forget to deal themselves into the game. And so, I help rebalance them and help them make time for themselves without feeling guilty. Often the women that I work with feel that they are being too selfish or believe "my needs don't count".

One of the common statements we work with them, and the horses is that "my needs count too". When the clients start to believe that their needs count too, the horse will start walking on more willingly with them. Supporting these go-getting women to find more balance helps them be more effective leaders and managers, run their business more successfully, improved family and relationships and most importantly more kind and loving relationship with themselves. The other type of women that come to me are often in that phase of life when they are coming up to the empty nest syndrome, or they want something a little bit more from their life, but not quite sure which way to go. Once again, the horses are fantastic for helping you find purpose and direction.

Cheryl Yeah, great, and I saw you recently speak at the International Women's Day event in Manchester. And I know there you shared a lovely, heart-breaking, and heart-warming story about how one of your clients, and I think this is a true testament to you, that she now actually works with you because she loved the fact that the horses helped her and now, she wants to help others. So, if people want to get in touch with you and or watch the video, honestly, watch the video of Wendy on stage, it's just incredible. There's a little secret at the beginning, but I'm not to spoil that for you. And so, if people want to get in touch with you and find out more about what you do, where can they get info?

Wendy Come along to *www.theheartcentreuk.com* that's where we'll give you details of one-day workshops. Or if you really want to transform your life then come on our HEART Self-mastery Through Horses course. That will guarantee to change your life (for the better). Or if you have teenagers or know of someone who has, that are struggling then visit *www.healingheartsandmindswithhorsescic.org*.

Cheryl Yeah. Brilliant, and we'll put the links below for both when this video on International Women's Day and of course that link for your website as well. But just one question before you go. And how did this all start?

Wendy Well, it all started with my childhood sweetheart, and I was 12 years old when I met him. And he was not very tall. He was dark, he was very handsome. It was my little pony called Tiggy, and that was over 50 years ago. He really did help me get through my childhood. And he was the catalyst of change. He taught me how to be in relationships, and what true unconditional love was, so much so that he was the inspiration for my first book, The Heart of Stable Relationships, 12 ways the Healing Power of horses can transform your life. He truly helped me change the lives of so many other people, too. I had the pleasure of 30 years with him.

Cheryl Aww bless, and you went on to write another book as well?

Wendy Yes, *I'm perfect as I am*, spelt I'm perfect as I am. And that is about how to break free from the prison of perfectionism because too many of us want to believe that we must get things perfect to be loved. And that's just not true.

Cheryl Brilliant. Wendy, thank you so much. Thank you for your amazing WHY's words on the couch today, but also for what you shared on stage so that thousands of others can see you and hear you and know that you are incredible, just as you are, of course. Thank you so much for the work that you do with people, specifically women, face to face, because, sometimes, you know, we can't remove our own appendix. And I'm not saying that Wendy will remove your appendix, sometimes you need somebody else to help you. So, I want to thank you so much for being you,and incredible we love you. And I hope everybody else will too, I'm sure they will.

Wendy Thank you, Cheryl, because it's with you that we've been able to achieve this.

Cheryl You're welcome. You're welcome. Thank you very much. For the next episode of WHY's Women sharing their WHY's words.

If you personally feel you could use some help from Wendy and the equine therapy, then you can contact Wendy directly on 07801 567850 or on these links

Links:
https://youtu.be/j4wSs2tzCFo
https://www.theheartcentreuk.com
https://www.linkedin.com/in/wendyfirminprice
https://www.healingheartsandmindswithhorsescic.org
wendy@theheartcentreuk.com
https://www.facebook.com/wendyfirminprice

See Wendy sharing her wisdom at The Confidently Come Speaking Lives in March 2023 via this

YouTube link: *https://youtu.be/j4wSs2tzCFo*

The final area that you may choose to be an Everyday Influencer and Confident Speaker is with your **Perspective**. What do I mean by perspective?

This could be because you don't have a product or service to sell to improve someone else's personal or professional lives. It could be because you want to share a different way to look at something – some information that you hope will help to enlighten the world.

Ordinarily, I would point you in the direction of TED.com because on this platform you are not allowed to openly sell, only share ideas. However, the ideas you share do have to be backed up by independent evidence and so if you don't fit into this category, you can share your beliefs in your own way by becoming part of our Everyday Influencers and the Confident Speakers community. Remember, we welcome anyone who wants to share how they Live, Love and Laugh every day.

"Everything you post on social media is your personal brand. How do you want to be known?"

Lisa Horne
a.k.a The Publicity Gal

CHAPTER 7

The Powerful Story Strategy™

Now you know your PURPOSE, with **The W.H.Y Finder Formula™** and your PROPOSAL using **The Successful Solution Framework™**

We can now start to move towards how you are going to POSITION yourself with **The Powerful Story Strategy™**

One of the fears my clients have is that they will be seen as showing off if they share all the success they have had in business, and this means that they don't want to be seen as self-promoting.

If you remember Helen Bartam from earlier.

The problem is that becoming the world's biggest secret is no good for you and your business and it's a problem for someone looking for a solution, if they can't find you.

Here is how to overcome the fear of showing off.

Make your story so relatable to the audience that they believe you are sharing their problem, their journey, and the happy ending that they are looking for. The most common words you will be using are you & yours not - me, myself, and I. This will create rapport and connection between you and your potential clients. Does that make sense? You may however, be thinking, how can my story relate to someone else's story if I don't know them?

The answer is to keep checking in with the audience and to make sure that this is at what is called "chunked up" in NLP, in simple terms, at a level that many will agree with you.

For example, in my story – I could ask the audience if they had 2 best friends called Gordon & Stella, who they spent every night with and who helped them to distract from a life where they worked for my ex-boss at my old company.

Can you see how there is no connection?

However, if I say my best friends were Gordon & Stella and if there was a 'y' in the day, I would be drinking both and then ask the audience

Have you ever used something to distract from your life, maybe alcohol, sex, drugs or sausage rolls, to numb the pain? Now this story is ideal for an audience who are looking to stop wasting their lives and are looking for a purpose.

How can you create a story like this?

Firstly, know thy audience – what pains do they have?

Now the tip is to find where in your life you had the same pains/ problem, and this will be a possible first scene in your story.

For the next part of the story - what have they tried and tested out to try to make these pains or problems go away?

The truth is your audience will more than likely be in this 2nd phase. That is, they are searching for a solution.

Here is where you take your experiences, what you tried – that failed or what you think they may try that won't work and this will make up the second scene. Notice that I say scenes – to recreate these, the scenes need to be 'seen' by the audience and this means you will need to describe the following:

PLACE – where are you in this scene?

PEOPLE – who are you with, what do they look like?

PROBLEM – what is the problem that needs to be revealed (please note through a conversation – not through narration)

Imagine we are watching the scene live.

As your storytelling skills become more advanced, you can add many details here. This is a simple structure to get you started. Here are the biggest lie people tell themselves when it comes to public speaking - people don't want to listen to stories.

If that was the case, no one would meet for coffee, or a chat and Netflix would be bust!

Stories are how we have shared knowledge since the beginning of time. Yes, there are ways of boring your audience and narration is one of them, however, you can also have too much detail and over the top acting and this is what spoils the delivery of a great story.

Imagine sitting in the pub and going into full Shakespeare mode. Yes, a little over the top at best!

And the length of the story has to be just right too.

I did build up a reputation for reducing stories down, like an editor leaving footage on the floor.

A tip is to have no more than 3 scenes in your positioning story to begin with, with practice you can start to have scenes within scenes, a little bit like a movie that time hops, this has to be created with precision to avoid confusion.

You can also have a client story, one that is not your own personal Hero's journey, one of your clients success, with your help of course!

However, unlike the movies, where your audience can be shown a scene where you are not there, to gleen information about the past. This can look odd at best when you are doing a 1 woman show! Instead reveal the problem in a scene with you.

In both cases the stories will finish with a happy ending, which is of course an example of what your client is wishing for in their life. The benefit with these stories is that the audience are rooting and cheering for you, because they want the same for themselves. The benefit therefore in either case is that the client can see your results from a place of being an expert to help them, not to big yourself up.

If you would like to watch more educational and entertaining (or as we call them Edutaining) videos – please use this link for The Confidently Come Speaking YouTube Channel:
https://youtu.be/gpmQsP2xk90

For my next client story, this lady had left a long-standing role in the NHS, and she knew she wanted to keep helping others, after all its in her blood! However, she wanted to move away from the politics of the workplace and came to me to create a framework to provide as an independent consultant. Rachael is a tissue viability specialist.

INTRODUCING INTERNATIONAL AWARD-WINNING SPEAKER AND EVERY DAY INFLUENCER

Rachael Franco

Here is the interview I did recently with Rachael. If you prefer to watch the video, please use this link: *https://youtu.be/fQNnXfV5iog*

Cheryl Today I am with an amazing woman. I've known her for a couple of years now. She just does incredible work out in the workplace and in people's lives. So please introduce yourself.

Rachael Hello, I'm Rachael Franco, and I'm a tissue viability educator and trainer specialising in pressure ulcer prevention and wound management.

Cheryl Brilliant. So, thank you for joining me here today. I know you've got like 300 years of experience that you could share with us today, but just in terms of what you do.

Rachael Tissue viability specialist just recently retired and now I'm forming my own business to set up an education and training business to help others, particularly healthcare organisations, to educate their staff on the dangers of pressure ulcers in their patients and clients.

Cheryl And why is that important for you to do that? What was the reason why you started to do this work in the first place?

Rachael Well, given that pressure ulcers are a hidden problem, I think it's important that this issue is made prominent in the public and that awareness is raised because it's estimated that over 700,000 people suffer from pressure ulcers in the UK. And it's estimated that between 4 and 10% of patients that are admitted to hospital suffer from pressure ulcers. So, they're not necessarily admitted to the hospital with the pressure ulcer, but it might be that they've been admitted for something else, and they just happened to have a pressure ulcer. So, it's important that this issue is made more prominent.

Cheryl Yeah, brilliant. And so, you were doing this in the NHS already? Yeah, and I know, you obviously understand why it's such a big issue. I heard you speaking recently saying that you went into hospital, and you sort of had this situation where you were like, oh my gosh, I need to do what I'm teaching to other people. What was that all about?

Rachael Yes. So I was on the other side, really. I was on the receiving end of care in the hospital, and I was recovering from major abdominal surgery. And when I came round, I was lying in the bed and I was aware that my heels were feeling quite sore, and it's probably because I've been in theatre on my back for quite a few hours and I realised that soreness and if something weren't done then I could get a pressure ulcer and I knew what to do because I was a health professional myself. So, I took action to try and relieve pressure by putting a pillow on my side.

Cheryl And so, it's just about information because it wasn't anything major that you needed to do, but if you hadn't known, it's kind of like saying, 'If you don't know what you don't know, you don't know it', right? And so, you also shared on that day about, you know, a patient that you were looking after, because obviously we think about pressure also and we think, you know, it's a bit like a blister or, you know, something that's a bit, you know, not a big issue, really. And yet you shared a story about a gentleman that you followed over several years, didn't you? Just to briefly share with the readers what happened there.

Rachael Well, this gentleman, when I first met him, he started off with a blister on his toe due to tight footwear, but he wasn't aware of it initially as he had diabetes, he lost sensation in his feet.

So, it was only when he saw a stain on his sock and that when I first set eyes on this patient, his wound had broken down. It clearly looked infected. Then over the next few years, that wound deteriorated. He kept getting repeated infections. He had to have his toe amputated, Then his foot and then part of his leg. All because of what started off as a simple little blister due to tight footwear, which was rubbing, and because he had diabetes that made him more prone to infection so it's very difficult for this wound to heal.

Cheryl Wow, and it's interesting because I know in the talk that you did on International Women's Day in Manchester, you started with, head, shoulders, knees, and toes. I mean, obviously, you were there to entertain the crowd and educate them at the same time because, you know, maybe people think it was a bit of a weird subject, why do I want to speak about pressure ulcers? But again, it's about educating people, isn't it? What was the reason for doing that at the beginning?

Rachael It's just to demonstrate to people that you don't only get pressure ulcers on one part of the body, such as the foot or wherever, you could get an ulcer anywhere, particularly on the bony prominences. So, I just demonstrated that you could get pressure ulcers on your ears. back of your head, your elbows and your hips, your knees. If you're an immobile patient that's got contracted legs and is reliant on carers, then you may not be able to relieve your own pressure and you may need help.

And it's also to enable people and their careers, if they do have carers, that those are the areas to look out for. And when that patient is being turned or they're having personal hygiene care, that it's important for the person that's helping them to look at those areas and for the patient to speak out as well and take responsibility for informing their carer member of the family that they are feeling quite sore. So, in a particular area say on the heels for instance so that further help can be obtained, same from the GP or the social services, whoever oversees that person's care if they are getting care from outside sources.

Cheryl And I believe that, you know when you're laughing, you can learn more. So, it was a great way to start your presentation. Yes. It was amazing to see you there and share it. And yet at the same time, it is a very serious situation. And so, the reason why you've created your new business after retiring, how long were you in the NHS? Did you say over 30 years?

Rachael Yes

Cheryl So, you're just getting used to it, but now you've started your consultancy and you can go into organisations. What type of organisations is it that you work with?

Rachael Well, I'm aiming my education and training at any healthcare establishment but mainly nursing homes, residential homes, care homes and the NHS, and anywhere where the staff may come across with people who are at risk of pressure, ulcers, people with chronic health conditions, for instance, or people who've got mobility problems because I've got so much information to share. I've got so much advice to give, and I'd like to be able to improve people's education and help them to deliver the best quality care possible in their organisation. So, I'm happy for any healthcare establishment to approach me and find out more.

Cheryl Because obviously, that means that there's not one of their members of staff doing the training. You come in, do the training, yeah, it helps everybody, it helps the situation. They get educated, but then you would leave and then go somewhere else. So, you're kind of flexible and moving around these organisations, is that right?

Rachael Yeah, yeah. So, I cover the Greater Manchester area, Merseyside, Lancashire, and Cheshire, so I'm happy to travel to those areas and do online training as well. But I think face-to-face training is particularly good because then you can involve the audience.

Cheryl Although you might not get them to do head shoulders, knees, and toes on this occasion. Do you want to share, Rachel, how people can get in touch with you and how these care homes and these organisations can reach you?

Rachael So, if you'd like to get in touch and know more about my business pressure learning and organise training for your staff, then I can be reached on Facebook. It's called Pressure

Ulcer Learning and my website 'pressureulcerlearning.com'. I've also got an email address as well. So, if you visit either the Facebook page or the website, then you can get in touch with me.

Cheryl Brilliant. And we'll pop the links below this interview. And of course, if you want to see Rachel's video in her presentation from International Women's Day in Manchester this year, then we'll also put the link to that so you can have a look at what she talks about. She's amazing, incredible. And thank you so much, Rachel, for sharing your wisdom not only with us today, but also throughout those 30 years and helping people, you know, to live healthier lives. So, thank you so much.

Rachael Nice to chat with you, thank you.

If you would like to get in touch or reach out to Rachael for assistance and information on Ulcer Care then you can do so at any of the following links

Email: *info@pressureulcerlearning.com*
Facebook: *https://www.facebook.com/pressureulcerlearning*
Website: *https://pressureulcerlearning.com*

See Rachael sharing her wisdom at The Confidently Come Speaking Live Event in March 2023 via this

YouTube link: *https://youtu.be/rvlYShZNAFY*

CHAPTER 8

The Authentic S.P.E.E.C.H Approach™

As well as having a structure to your presentation with **The Powerful Story Strategy™** there is another element to introduce that I use side by side when guiding the Everyday Influencers to create their presentations and that is the piece that helps them to PREPARE. The strategy here is **The Authentic S.P.E.E.C.H Approach™**.

In order to deliver a presentation, you need to know more than the words you need to speak to them out loud!

I know this may sound a little bit facetious, but it's not intended in this way. However, have you ever said something in your head, maybe rehearsing what you were going to say to a partner, boss, or teacher and well at the time of delivery it all gets mixed up and comes out completely wrong? Yep, that's because it was only said inside your head or out loud on your own.

There are 4 elements to this approach. The first is something you can do on your own and that is to **Record** yourself doing your presentation. It doesn't have to be anything fancy at this stage as it is only for practice. However, I would say make sure you practice in the way that it will be delivered. If you are going to present sitting down, do the recording sitting down. If you will be standing up, then make sure you record standing up, so you are replicating the end delivery style.

The next stage can begin with you and that is to Review the recording. Here you want to review this in two distinct ways:

1. Review as a member of your potential audience. Embody your client and review what you are saying and how you look would you resonate with you?
   Do you look nervous? Are you making eye contact? Are you being natural? Would you feel like you know, like and trust you after watching you?
2. This is a little trickier as you need to review yourself in an impartial way and as a mentor would. How can you improve the presentation? Can you move elements around? What needs to change to make your presentation skills even better? There is a tendency here to show a member of your family or friend the video and ask for feedback.

This is ok if they are trained in this area. Otherwise, it's a sensitive situation in the making! They are not trained, you may disagree with their thoughts, or even more dangerously they may not want to give you the feedback they would if you weren't you. Have you ever watched a reality show like X-Factor and thought, "do these people live alone - who actually told them they could sing? Do they not have any friends or family to tell them the truth?" And then Simon Cowell says what most of the audience are thinking and you squirm in your seat.

This is what you are potentially setting yourself up for. The feedback has to be honest and encouraging with some ideas on how to improve the presentation. Like I said in the case of the TED talks, it is my reputation on the line as well as yours and so for both our sakes I will give you my true feedback and highlight where and how the presentation can be made even better. Here you must be able to **Revise** the presentation with these guidelines and repeat the above 3 steps, until you get the sign off that you are good to go.

Now it is about the final part, and this is really up to you. Even when you work with me, you have to put the time to **Rehearse**. Practice, practice, practice the agreed presentation. Not memorise, practice. In the shower, in the bath, walking the dog, around the house, into your phone - practice out loud! Here, when I run the WHYs Word events, for those people willing to travel to me, we have a full-dress rehearsal too so you know where you are going to stand and where the cameras are, and you can deliver with a small audience.

This means that when you come to do your presentation, you've already done it so many times that it is familiar. It's also a great time to try out the outfit you want to wear, instead of realising that it doesn't feel comfortable on the day of delivery.

I remember when Avie came to a dress rehearsal, we offer this service, so that the speakers get the opportunity to deliver their presentation from start to finish. Avie is an accomplished trainer and union representative, with no problems voicing her opinion. However, speaking on a stage in front of an audience requires a different set of skills.

Avie had created a good story, however, here at Confidently Come Speaking we don't do "good". I helped Avie to create an outline of a story in 7 minutes, yes with over a decade of experience I can do this!! Maybe you have years of experience that means you can achieve something in a fraction of the time that someone learning the skill can.

Avie left with a storyboard and a recording and set to work.

The day after her story was transformed and there was not a dry eye in the house. We had been able to incorporate all the key elements of her story into a compelling expert positioning story.

INTRODUCING INTERNATIONAL AWARD-WINNING SPEAKER AND EVERYDAY INFLUENCER

Avie Kaur

Avie Kaur is a teacher and an advocate for change Here is the interview I did recently with Avie at The Confidently Come Speaking Live in March 2023.

If you prefer to watch the video, please use this link: *https://youtu.be/0_NnMBfMNlk*

Cheryl Today, an incredible woman is joining me on the couch. She is Wow, what can I say? Very educational. That's going to give a little bit away. So please introduce yourself.

Avie Hello, my name is Avie Kaur. I am a teacher and I enable people to learn all kinds of things.

Cheryl In terms of what they learn, obviously you've been a teacher in a traditional sense, if you like, but also a teacher for clarity, what is it that you help people get clarity around?

Avie I help people find clarity around where they are right now in life, whether they want to change work, whether they want to be re-educated, maybe they want to go back and do that degree they never did. But also, to help them see if they are in the right place for them right now.

Cheryl You're wearing a traditional dress today, and I know that you said before, there was a little bit of a conundrum, do you wear this dress, or do you wear a non-traditional dress? Just share what was going on before.

Avie So, the panic was when people see me in traditional dress, they have certain beliefs. Am I going to be suitable for what they're looking for? And usually, does she speak English? And so, it's just really to get over to people that whatever we look like, we should always be our authentic selves and present ourselves as we feel happy to. When I'm in class, this is very rare, so, when I'm talking with clients and people who I know, I'm not usually dressed like this, but it is good for them to see that I do have that other side to me. And it helps people who are from my background to be thinking, wow, I can do this too.

Cheryl It's amazing. Recently you did an event, you were at an event at International Women's Day in Manchester, and you were speaking on the stage, and you came on doing a traditional dance as well. That was brilliant because the whole audience was clapping and dancing along with you as well, which was a great way to start your presentation. But really there were some, or should I say, some bigger messages that were going on there that weren't there? What were you sharing on that day?

Avie I think it's about sharing the important things about being yourself because culture has a massive role to play for a lot of people. And I think for women, we're bound not just by culture, but we are bound by tradition. So, when you come from other backgrounds, the tradition and the culture can be a double whammy. So, allowing women to sort of stand up and say, "Actually, this is who I am", you know it's important to embrace both those sides of yourself and feel that you're comfortable doing whatever you do because, underneath it all, you're still you.

Cheryl I know you developed a program to help your potential clients, didn't you? It's got quite an apt name If I remember rightly.

Avie Well, being a teacher, I've just simply called it 'The Putting It to The Test Program'. It literally does what it says on the tin. It's about testing yourself, about where you are, what are you doing, what you would like to be. We go through all those conundrums that we get in later life, like when you hit 30, and you think "Is this all there is?" And so, it's really to explore those things through the program.

Cheryl So, if somebody is listening now to this video, what might be going on in their life right now that you could help them with?

Avie Oh, recent inquiries have been things like "I've just had a baby, but I don't want to go back to where I used to work, and I don't think I've got any other skills, so, what could I do instead? And the common one, when I used to work with teachers predominantly was "I've been a teacher all my life, what else can I do? I don't know how to do anything else". So, it's exploring those things, what do you want to do, you know, what was it that led you to do what you're doing already and why don't you like it now? We sometimes have that decision about what we want to do made for us, and it's to please other people often. And then you get to that point in life where you think, "Well, I've done it for X number of years and now I can't do it anymore because it's not me and it doesn't feel right anymore". And at that point is where I can step in and say, well, let's look at where you are and what skills you've got and what other jobs are there out there that would be really, more suitable. So that's the point of the program, it is to bring that clarity to people and help them along the way to maybe develop some of those skills that they might need to take that next step.

Cheryl Brilliant. And so, the clarity on maybe their career, the clarity on who you really are and obviously like you've just said Avie, as time passes, we change. Everything's constantly changing so, you can help them with the clarity of knowing where to go next. I know at the International Women's Day you launched your book didn't you? Tell us a little bit about your book?

Avie So, the book is your fault, Cheryl. So, the book really was all my life. I've sort of written things down because, for me, journaling was the only way to keep a tab on my thoughts. And so over time, they just became long narrative poems, and it's been helpful in terms of trying to find which ones to put in the book. And so, then I thought, well, as it's a journey that I've been on, it's a journey that I can help other people to go on to realise that sometimes the issues that we have now may well begin way back when we were younger. So that's why my story began from when I was so small to where I am now because again, it's all about communication. And so, the journey of self-realisation from being called her to not being me myself, is what led me to, sort of be where I am today. And that's why the book reflects that, that there's this whole journey we go on. And all through life you have those as you so aptly put them, sometimes you have those hiccups in life that you know, you think, oh my God, I can't get past this. I don't know what I'm going to do next. But having that resilience to be able to say, okay, this is what I want to do, this is who I am, and this is where I need to be. And that sort of pushes you along and that makes you move, take that step forward. Knowing when you can rely on yourself, but also when to ask for help, because so many of us just don't ask for help because we don't know where to go for help.

Cheryl And that little sense of like, oh, if I ask for help, I might be vulnerable. And obviously, we know that vulnerability is a strength, not a weakness.

That vulnerability is a strength, not a weakness.

And it's great to read the book because even though it's poems and poetry and prose of your life, there are so many similarities for you and your potential clients Oh, my gosh. So, you kind of turned into your own therapist if you like. Or is your own therapy by writing the prose? And now you can help other people in a similar situation, too, which is great.

Avie What was wonderful about the International Women's Day presentation and then the one I did sort of a bit later was literally the women coming up to me, afterwards. saying, oh my God, that happened to me. I can remember when somebody made a choice for me that I didn't want to make. And it was the Asian women who sort of came and said, oh my God, I've just seen me. I've seen somebody who looks like me. And I think the power is in knowing that what you see there represents who you are.

In class, I always used to say, if you can't see it, you can't be it. And so, this is what I'm trying to put out there now that you can see it, so therefore, you can be.

Cheryl Brilliant. Thank you so much, Avie. Thank you for sharing your wisdom on the stage. Thank you for sharing your wisdom in your book and for being here. And if you'd like to connect with Avie, if there's just something that she said today, where you go, I think that could be me.

Avie I have a website called www.teachingmentoringcoaching.com and you can find me on there. I'm on LinkedIn and you can find me on Facebook @avietmcfacebook.

Cheryl Brilliant. So, thank you so much, Avie. Thank you for all the work that you've done over the years with the children and obviously with the women. And I know that there's lots more that you can find out about, like why she was doing driving instruction and oh, you name it, like in the past. So please connect with Avie. Look at her video from International Women's Day as well. It's just amazing to see her dancing on stage and connecting with the audience and hopefully, you will find something that she can help you with, too. Thank you so much.

Avie Thank you.

Cheryl We'll see you soon. Next time for the next WHY's words.

If you would like to contact Avie for any further details, then please do so at the following.
https://youtu.be/VUCqTL-521Y
https://teachingmentoringcoaching.com
https://www.facebook.com/AvieTMC
https://www.linkedin.com/in/avie-kaur-coach-mentor-teacher

See Avie sharing her wisdom at The Confidently Come Speaking Live in March 2023 via this

YouTube link: *https://youtu.be/VUCqTL-521Y*

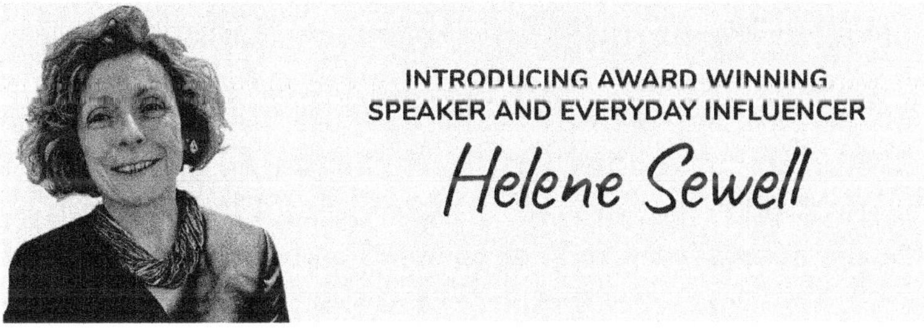

Helen was another speaker and successful business owner who wanted to reach more clients. However, she had fallen into the trap of believing that when speaking to a business client, she couldn't share emotion in her story and that meant her story came across as cold.

Adding in just the right amount of emotion led to clients who had previously walked away from Helene's services, come back to engage her to help grow their business.

The reason being, she was authentic, and they knew her purpose, the reason why she went into business.

Here is the interview I did recently with Helene at The Confidently Come Speaking Live in March 2023. If you prefer to watch the video, please use this link: *https://youtu.be/kJvOB3iT4wY*

Cheryl Hello and welcome to WHY's Words, where I'm interviewing WHY's women, women who found their WHY, their passion, their purpose, and who are sharing their wisdom about who they are and the amazing work that they're doing in the world right now. Today, this lovely lady I've only known for a few months, but, you know, when you just see somebody, and you know that they know what they know, and you know that they are in action and they're helping others. So please introduce yourself.

Helene Well, I'm Helene Sewell and I am a business navigator. It means that I'm a business mentor and I help business owners and entrepreneurs, most of them are neurodiverse, succeed in their business endeavours.

Cheryl Brilliant. And for those who don't understand what neurodiverse is, what is neurodiverse?

Helene Well, there's many flavours of neurodiversity, but, you know, a lot of them will be either ADHD, dyslexic, autistic, to name a few.

Cheryl And do you find that the creative side is brilliant with the people that you work with? What do you normally find about them that you like working with?

Helene Well, what I like about entrepreneurs and a lot of neurodiverse entrepreneurs is the passion they have for what they do, a desire to do things properly, you know, not half-heartedly. So generally, their business is way more than just a way of earning a living. There will be passion, a push behind it and a tendency to think outside the box and come up with ideas for their business to actually serve, you know, their customer in a special way.

Cheryl Great. and why are you so passionate about helping people in business?

Helene Um, well, it really comes from my childhood because I was brought up on a farm and a farm is a business. And both my mom and dad worked on the farm, one very successfully and the other one less so. And I started to learn lessons from there. But the first lesson I learned was that if I want to take charge of my life, entrepreneurship is by far the best route.

Cheryl Yeah, brilliant. I know recently you shared that story. You shared that on International Women's Day in Manchester. And you know, you could hear a pin drop, when you shared about your mum and her passion and your dad, obviously, and your brother as well. If you'd like to see that video, we will put the link below. So I don't want to give away too much right now, but I think it really showed that your passion, you know, for what you do, you know, the reason why you want to help so many other people is once you realised that it was your WHY if you like, you know your purpose, that it really gave you that power to go forward. Would you say that's true?

Helene Yeah, absolutely. I mean, I've spent 25 years working in businesses, and I've always been very curious as to what makes them work and what doesn't and what makes them fail. And I just love to help people succeed, especially when they have, a passion and they want to serve some specific people who might have specific challenges.

If they have a greater purpose, a good cause that they want to serve with their business, then they must succeed. And I see so many failures in business and I know how to make business succeed. So, I should help them.

Cheryl And in terms of the businesses that you're helping, are they new businesses, are they well established? What kind of businesses do you help?

Helene There isn't really a stage. Some of my clients are not even in business yet and are thinking of going into business. And some of them have been going for a long time. I mean, I've got a lady I've just started working with, been going for 14 years, so it's not what stage they are in business. It's about, are they stuck in their business, do they feel overwhelmed, are they lacking direction, or do they have a real ambitious goal that they want to achieve because they've got something to give to the world and they don't know how to get there, and that's what I can help them with.

Cheryl Yeah, and I know you were saying just recently that you started to help somebody and obviously it's about return on your investment, isn't it in business? So, you'd helped her, already to find quite a big saving in her business?

Helene Yeah, well if the business is already going then you know, one of the first things I will do is go through their numbers, look at their finances. I'm an accountant by training, so that's something I know very, very well.

And I will undoubtedly find some way I can save them some money and then they start to get a return on investment, not even considering the growth that I can help them achieve in their business. I will help them pay for the mentoring investment, through the savings straight from the off.

Cheryl Brilliant, it's like a quick win, and then you're helping them to build the business, grow the business etc.

Helene Because a lot of what I do is long term, but I can also bring benefits short term, and I'll do both, of course.

Cheryl Yeah, brilliant. And on that International Women's Day, I know that you shared a process, you know, a strategy that you've got if I remember right, it's the 4 P's.

Helene Yes, that's right.

Cheryl Is that what you use with your clients?

Helene Yes, very much so. It is a framework. It's not a rigid process. But what I've learned in all the years I've worked in businesses is that there are certain elements that need to be in place in a business and without them, which then you significantly increase your chances of failure. And to make it easy, yes, I called it "The Thriving Business Tool Kit". And it all starts with P's. There's P for The Big Picture, you know, what is the identity of your business?

A business that doesn't have an identity will lose itself along the way. The second P is for Particulars, and that's because every business is different. There will be things that make that business tick that are different from another business and understanding exactly what are those particulars that need to be looked after is very important. The third P is for Planning because we all know that a goal without a plan is just a wish. And I can help plan about everything that you need to plan in the business, money, strategy, resources. And the fourth one then, allows them to grow the business to wherever they want to get to. And that's P for Power Up, which is how to delegate, how to have a training program for yourself and your team, and how to have a dashboard that supports the business in those areas of growth.

Because it's a quite vulnerable time for business when you grow rapidly, there's lots of things are changing. So how do you make sure that you've got your attention on the right things so that you know it's not going off kilter when it's quite vulnerable?

Cheryl Yeah, yeah, brilliant. And so, if there's somebody out there that's, you know, stuck, maybe fallen out of passion with their business or thinking of starting a business and they don't know what to do, how can they contact you? How can they connect with you?

Helene I'm quite easy to find. I have a website and that's *www.the-business-navigator.com*. But you can also find me on LinkedIn and it's easy to find me because I'm the only one with the spelling of my name on LinkedIn. That's Helene Sewell, there's only one in the UK with that spelling. That's probably the easiest way to find me on LinkedIn or the website.

Cheryl Brilliant, we'll pop the links underneath this video. And if you want to find out how you can either start a business, that comes from passion, or if you've got a business right now that you want to grow and scale, then I hope that you'll connect with Helene. And so, we want to say thank you so much. Thank you, Helene, for everything that you're doing in the world of business. It's a tough, you know, a tough place to be. I think you shared a statistic on how many businesses don't survive. Do you remember how many there where?

Helene Yeah, absolutely. 60% of businesses will fail in the first three years, and only about 40% of businesses that are put up for sale will get sold for an amount. So, that means that only one in nine entrepreneurs will leave a legacy. And to me, that's a crime.

Cheryl Yeah. So, if you'd like to increase that number so that your business survives and thrives, then this is the lady to connect with. Thank you for everything that you do. Thank you for sharing your wisdom and we will see you soon on the next episode of The WHY's Words.

If you are wanting more information or wanting to connect with Helene on how you can improve your business, you can connect with Helene here
https://youtu.be/Xu9w1ODH114
https://www.the-business-navigator.com
https://www.facebook.com/The.Business.Navigation.Centre
https://www.linkedin.com/company/the-business-navigation-centre
https://www.instagram.com/tbnc_businesstips

See Helene sharing her wisdom at The Confidently Come Speaking Event in March 2023 via this YouTube link:
https://youtu.be/Xu9w1ODH114

CHAPTER 9

The S.I.L.V.E.R. Screen Star Principles™

By now you will be aware of who, what and why you want to be a Freedom Speaker and Everyday Influencer. Someone who supports others with your products, services or ideas in a way that means that your potential clients see that you can help them in areas of their lives so that they can achieve their purpose in life (which I personally think is to be happy. You know what is needed to be able to connect in terms of a presentation, i.e., what needs to be covered and how to improve it. So now, in this section, how can you bring all of that together to PROMOTE yourself and your personal brand, so people get to know, like and trust you?

The S.I.L.V.E.R. Screen Star Principles™ was developed based on what helped me to be seen, heard and felt and this came from being around successful speakers who were seen as the celebrities, authorities and experts in their areas of expertise the go-to people.

At the time of writing this book, the world has changed. Social distancing has meant that we don't get big crowds anymore and 'pivoting' became the new word for 2020, with most face-to-face businesses 'pivoting' online.

Entrepreneurs, employers, employees, and enlightened souls were all looking for ways to connect. Clubhouse became the new way to do this through the medium of sound only, Instagram focused on pictures, Facebook used words and images, and YouTube utilised videos. Webinars became as common as Zoom meetings and interviews.

As we sat in our 'safe houses' we still wanted to be connected it's what being a human is all about, right?

As mentioned before, the mind loves the familiar and TV stations used this by creating entertainment shows with distancing and no audiences (but they did have recorded laughter and clapping). Sports started again with no crowds, but they did have cut outs and recorded crowd sound.

We started to feel involved again.

Could we use this principle as an Everyday Influencer too? Let's see, if you were to attend a webinar or see an advert on social media where there was a product or a service on offer that you liked the sound of (that would be useful for you) and you wanted to find out about the person/company selling this solution for you, where would you look? I imagine you'd do a Google search, check out the website, search for reviews, or scroll through social media, right?

And what if you were able to see that they were professional, personable and you could see, hear and feel them? Would it be fair to say that you would only investigate their offer more if you got to know, like and trust them? With **The S.I.L.V.E.R. Screen Star Principles™** it's about lights, camera and action. What can you do to increase your star quality? And by that, I'm talking about what people see when they look for you and where are they going to find you?

Let's take a look at how you can PROMOTE yourself by looking at the 6 principles in this strategy. If you want to be seen as an Everyday Influencer, you still need positioning, and a great place to start is being seen, heard and felt from a **STAGE**. Showing the world that you are able to stand up and share what you believe and know, will help to position you (remember a lot of people are afraid of speaking in public).

Being able to show you are able to do this in itself gains you some 'brownie points' and helps you to be seen as a leader/influencer when you speak from any kind of stage (this could also be an online platform too). Companies, of course, spend millions on adverts on TV, which is their stage.

You can reach out to promoters who run events where you will pay to appear on stage. Or you can put your own events on where the expense is covered by you, and you get speakers to pay to speak on your stage. The key here is, even if you can't have a large crowd, you still dress the stage accordingly backdrops, props and a setting worthy of the thousands of people who will see the recording. This is why a Zoom recording doesn't compare. Where do you find film stars, musicians, authors when they want to promote their products?

That's right. Chat shows where the hosts like Graham Norton, Loose Women, and Jonathan Ross **INTERVIEW** the guests to help promote their new offering without sounding salesy. And we love to see these stars in a setting where we get to know some secrets about them and see them in a relaxed state - like we are sitting on the sofa next to them.

Even in the times of the pandemic, stars were seen sitting 2m away from each other in the studio – no audience, just the celebs and the host. Why? Because the Zoom interviews didn't work as well as the 'in the room' ones - they felt a bit 2D, a bit flat (see what I did there, I know you may be thinking, "don't start clowning around, Cheryl!")

You can reach out to people you see who are interviewing in your sphere of influence or you can pay someone to interview you. It's better to have a trained interviewer as you may find your friend or family member dries up too quickly! It's an added bonus if the person interviewing can sell too as that way, they can promote your product or service for you. With these 2 simple steps you start to be seen on a professional as well as on a personal level. Therefore, strangers literally get to know you in a much shorter space of time while you are positioning yourself as a person with integrity and solutions that they could benefit from.

By recording the presentation and interview, you can now share these videos on your website, YouTube and/or on social media, so that you can be found when someone Googles you Here, I want to point out that, in order to be seen as a professional, it is worth making sure that the videos you are posting to position yourself are not the Facebook Live, handheld smart phone recorded ones.

While these definitely have a place in your connection with your audience/clients, it's just not here!

LIGHTING and a **VIDEOGRAPHER** that will capture you from 2 angles and the latter must have the capacity to become the **EDITOR** of the footage to make a showreel, promotional presentation or just make you look like the professional you are. I cannot stress how important it is to get a professional here and not someone who takes pictures as a hobby, as the penny pinching will only result in poor quality videos.

And when you find a great one, keep hold of them.

Rebecca Andrews, who does all the filming at my events, was the videographer responsible for all the TEDxAinleyTopWomen filming and so we adopted the same standards for The WHYs Words filming too. Top quality! Thank you, Rebecca!

Finally, when you have your recordings, you need to **RELEASE** them into the world. What I mean here is, get a buzz going, contact the local press to run a story for you and get others to like and share to their friends, relatives, work colleagues. Repeat this process to get some leverage through social media and of course on your website/ landing page. As a footnote, if you want to create all this as a stage for you or for others too, you need to be resourceful and have assistance. For The Confident Come Speaking Events I have an incredible team including Jane Leonard, my Confident Business partner, Nilam Dattani, who looks after anything organisational including coordination of the speakers, and Gemma Brooks, my P.A.

When you are creating a video of your presentation and interview it is better to invest in a professional It's time to show how you are a Confident Speaker and that you help others as the Everyday Influencer that you are. The world needs you to help those who are in need of what you already know. If you'd like some more support. And if you'd rather leave all the planning to us, I'm always looking for entrepreneurs, employees, employers, and enlightened souls to share their WHYs Words.

Connect with me for a strategy call by email to
cheryl@cheryl-chapman.com

There is a thought that I'd like to share with you, which I share with The Confidently Speaking community.

There are 3 days that are important in your life: the day you are born, the day you find your WHY and the last time someone mentions your name (the latter is estimated somewhere around 3 generations after you've left this life).

Speaking has been a way for me to connect with the living and it also has helped me keep alive the essence of my cousin Lynsey, who died at the young age of 27 leaving behind her son Jordan. She had a mantra which was to choose 5 minutes of wonderful, rather than a life of regret

And she wanted her son to Live Love and Laugh every day.

Dedicated to Lynsey and her memory.

What will you be remembered for?

Will it be for guiding others, for standing up and speaking out, for being a freedom speaker or an everyday influencer?

Will you leave a legacy in the form of the results you helped others with? Will others sit and watch your videos and say, "look this is your ancestor and look how they helped the world and the people in it?" I know you have everything you need to do this - it's time to be seen, heard and felt

In closing, here is our final Everyday Influencer and Award Winning Speaker, a woman who has dared to be different all her life. I invite you to see how she can even get passionate about death.

INTRODUCING FREEDOM SPEAKER AND EVERYDAY INFLUENCER

Dr. Dawn Gibbins MBE

Dr. Dawn Gibbins MBE has been voted more influential than Sir Richard Branson and James Dyson, as well as 'Veuve Clicquot Businesswoman of the year'. She founded, built and sold her global environmental transformation company for millions and has appeared on the Channel four programme 'The Secret Millionaire' twice. Dawn is a woman who 'Dares to be Different'. She used Feng Shui to transform her business from a loss to a five-million-pound profit in three years, increasing team happiness from sixty per cent to ninety per cent at the same time. Universities have awarded Dawn doctorates for her tireless passion to empower people, make a difference, and help to create a better world.

She is a vibrant, energetic and a heartfelt public speaker, inspiring global audiences with her colourful, creative, courageous and unique style.

Here is the interview I did recently with Dawn at The Live Love Laugh Lives. If you prefer to watch the video, please use this link: *https://youtu.be/jbXUYG28t4k*

Dawn I started the business in 1982 and then by the time I flogged it many years later I made a lot of money, and also made five other people millionaires. This was in the year of 2008.

Cheryl Wow! I can still remember the first time we met, and you had the same bright orange colour hair you've got now - always one to stand out from the crowd!
We were at a speaker event in London, and you came in and the vibe was very much like – whoa she has arrived! You had incredible energy and presence about you. We managed to have a little conversation and a chat, and you excitedly asked me if you could do my 'numbers'. At the time all I can remember thinking is "what is she on about and is she some kind of quirky bingo caller or something?" I really had no idea what on earth was going on or what you were referring too but I played along, and you got very passionate telling me I was a 959! Like "oh my gosh you're a 959!"

Dawn Yes, so let me explain why I got so fired up talking about numbers! When I was running my company, I had five hundred staff to look after, which is a huge responsibility and commitment. At one point we lost a lot of money, and I was like "oh heck what am I going to do?"
We lost half a million pound in one year! So, the year prior I'd been learning personally all about Feng Shui. What I was learning was mind-blowing - the ways that Feng Shui can transform your life, your business and your community.
There is an element in there regarding a particular nine number and this is what I was referring to. This book here which I've brought along with me is all about Feng Shui Astrology. It is very worn and tatty because over the last twenty years and all through my business career, in the end, it's been a very precious tool, insight and guiding light for me.
I used this book to help me analyse people when I was recruiting and in the process of developing teams together as it's so essential to get the right people working together to maximise the best results, performance, and environment.

The really huge and impactful thing for me regarding these numbers was using them to really help me to tune in and listen and work with all I was learning. To develop myself and be in tune with the energy around me, to trust it and begin co-creating with it, to really open my heart and feel and trust the unseen forces which we often overlook. It was fascinating and exciting using this new learning and watching as life unfolded in- credibly and it's why I still get so giddy and excited about it to this very day.

It kind of evolved over about five years or so. I was running the business and I was doing so with my husband alongside me. I'd recruited him and made him a sales director. I looked at both our numbers collectively and I saw that a few years into the future I was going to be in my nine number (a fire year) - a year which symbolised fame and abundance. So, I thought, "my goodness, if we're going to sell this business, that's the year we need to do it." It transpired that my husband was in a great year also then as well and the year was 2008. So, yeah, I used the numbers to look at the energy of the year and what it meant for us and the business. These numbers are derived from the energy of time when you were born and there is so much wisdom and knowledge to be gained from studying it and paying attention.

From this information that I use. I can also find out so much about you - what your purpose, passion and power is. So, by studying and knowing these things it means that every year you can find out what energy you are in, so you can make the most of your life, basically, with feng shui astrology you use it to live your best life joyfully and I find it so wonderfully exciting.

Cheryl So, it sounds like you use it very much like it's like a guide then? I imagine that there are some people who would think, oh it's just way too 'woo woo' and far out there for me, stuff like that – as maybe I did a little at first if I'm totally honest. However, I now speak from experience and can say the amount of times that we've had conversations and then things have happened afterwards as a result of me listening, being open-minded and implementing changes. I know there's a little voice that says "Well, it's just coincidence and if you think something good's going to happen and you tell yourself it's so then maybe it will be," but there have just been too many examples now.

One example I can give is when you did some feng shui on a previous house I lived in. My husband was working away and so we had a free run of the house, and you asked me what I thought about one particular room in the house. It was like a little extra room off the kitchen and I said to you "it's got nothing to do with me as I don't use it."

What you said next to me was fascinating as you then told me this was in fact my wealth room. My initial reaction was, oh here she goes with all the 'woo woo' stuff! But I played along as we looked around the room - a black and white, very macabre room that consisted of dead iconic individuals such as Marilyn Monroe and other images such as Boudicca women figurines surrounded by skulls. Not a vibrant alive room at all - more like a scene from a night with the living dead! I had to chuckle as it spelt death and decay - a far cry from the feeling and picture of life, wealth, and abundance!

Dawn One other thing I noticed was that in this zone, your abundance zone which is in the Southeast area of your home is that you had no plants. You had a really great window but there was no greenery and no signs of growth or life. So straight away I was visualising bamboo growing and flowing in the wind, letting the air and nature in, welcoming and attracting abundance to you and my imagination was going wild just witnessing the unused potential of your home and living space.

Cheryl Yes, I remember but what we did have was a spiky plant and you noticed it and said to me, "oh, money in, money out." Now, at the time, I'd just in the last twelve months set up my business and I'll be honest I had more money in my accounts than I'd ever had before. So, I was like, "oh, bless her."

However, about three days later, Marion, my business partner, was staying with me and I received a corporation tax bill.

Something I didn't even know existed or that I had to pay - that's how new all this was to me. To cut a long story short it wiped out all the accounts I had. So, as you so rightly said "money in, money out!" So, things were really starting to get my attention now. Needless, to say the plant got dug up and thrown over the bloody fence!

The wallpaper came off and I began emptying the dead room immediately. When Marion came down-stairs, I think she thought I had lost the plot!

Dawn Honestly as much as we are laughing about this now, it's really moving for me to hear you sharing the impact it has made on you. Because you were open-minded and so willing to try out new concepts and ideas. The fact, Cheryl, that you were willing to listen to me and get out of your mind literally!

The transformation has been simply amazing. All the dark Marilyn Monroe design was removed and replaced with bamboo wallpaper, which looked incredible. Then you moved a table in there for yourself to take full advantage of the room. One of the huge things in any endeavour is action. You need action, you need movement, you need dancing, you need communication, you need energy, as they say, "you've got to be in it to win it!"

I could tell you meant business and we're embracing it all with gusto and such fabulous energy, a winning combination, and I'm just so proud of you.

You literally got into action straight away from that table - a workspace for you to communicate and reach out to people in your business, as you began to witness things begin to grow and flourish.

Cheryl Thank you. It really has been an incredible journey. Also, I remember that you gave me three little money plants. This is one of those not so little plants now (points to a huge plant to the left of her chair). I've just kept moving it and repotting it as it continues to grow and multiply! There really has been so much growth and abundance that has begun to flow and open up to us since implementing these small changes which, with hindsight, seem so obvious. True what they say about, it's the simple things that we overlook. It's also helped us to grow the business, which is doing very well. Also, since then as you know, we have moved house to a bigger, spacious, and very beautiful location that we had envisaged and have been able to make it our reality both for our personal living space and a perfect home to grow and support the business and events we hold. So, I cannot tell you how grateful I am, and what it has done for me and those who I work with; with whom I share and pass on all I have learnt and continue to do so from all you share. So, thank you, Dawn. Now I would love to talk to you about Dawn, the amazing businesswoman. As I said earlier the first time I met you, my first impression was you were a bit crazy and very different. Yet in such a beautiful way. You have such a magnetic aura, and your energy is so beautiful and vivacious. You are the sort of person that when you walk into a room, you light it up to the point where you need shades!

When you arrive, everybody feels it and is aware of the change in the atmosphere in a very positive way. But your talents don't stop there because even in such a male-dominated industry at a time where there was only you and only one other woman riding the wave, you were winning awards. Could you tell us a bit more about these?

Dawn Yes of course. Basically, as I mentioned earlier, I was in construction and manufacturing, and I was always in the newspapers because I was a woman working in this field. One year, the manufacturing magazine decided to look for the most influential person in British manufacturing as a way to celebrate and boost Britain and British manufacturing. So, they created the Manufacturing Power Fifty awards. It was voted for by all manufacturers and people within the industry. And Cheryl, I am so proud of this one which I have with me today because I won! There were only two women in the whole of the Power Fifty awards. So, who did I beat? I beat Sir Richard Branson (he came second) and James Dyson who came fourth. So why did I win? Well, I feel it's because when I meet people, I see the spirit of who they are within, all they are capable of, and I want to inspire those people. So, I look, watch, listen and use Feng Shui in my business and particularly in the manufacturing environments in as many ways as I can. Yes, I'm very aware that at first people thought I was a bit bonkers, because I don't follow the well-trodden path or expectations. My manufacturing site had great big pictures of tropical beaches, forests, rivers and nature all over them. A lot of manufacturing premises do not have a lot of natural daylight. They have windowless walls, so you've got to bring the beautiful light in. You've got to bring beautiful pictures in to inspire, energise, uplift and awaken our spirits. So that's what I was all about. I truly care about people and their well-being. So, my numbers are six to nine. I'm a leader, guide and mentor. But my two represents the carer inside of me. I care so deeply about people. My nine number is on the outside - meaning what I'm physically doing and putting into action, and this is your core number. I just love to illuminate and light people up from within. So, I was doing this within my field, illuminating the manufacturing industry and then the construction business. But beating Sir Richard Branson and James Dyson was a very proud moment and is definitely my claim to fame!

Cheryl Absolutely and rightly so! So now that we know you are no longer in manufacturing (as you shared with us earlier) as you sold the business for an undisclosed figure (which people can find out on Google if they wanted to!!!), you've now moved and are living in a place where I've had the privilege to visit and it's called...wait for it...'Bliss Land' and it's just amazingly fabulous! I remember getting a little lost trying to find it until I came to a point in the road where I could see a huge bear appearing and I thought, this has got to be it - only you Dawn! So, tell us about Bliss Land, what are you doing now? what does it stand for? and what is your new mission and purpose in helping others?

Dawn Well, there are three key areas that I'm focusing on my life right now. My third act, as I like to call it. From me being sixty to the day I die is to basically leave a legacy. And I can summarise it with three B's - bears, bliss and burials. My beautiful husband and I are setting up a charity called 'Return to Nature' with this in mind. So, let me explain. First, of all bears. Next year, which is 2021, is the Tenth anniversary of an event called Bear Mania. We had a big cultural arts festival that all came from Feng Shui, from doing a Feng Shui survey on the town of Congleton.
So that's where the bears came from.
Basically, Feng Shui stated to resurrect the spirit of the bear so that's what we did, and I've decided to launch again next year and every year. So, I'm now known as the 'bear woman' in Congleton!
So, what's the importance of bears you might be thinking and what is its relevance? Bear in my book stands for branding and enriching, awakening and reviving people and places, bringing things back to life with renewed energy and love. So that's my first B. Moving now onto 'Bliss', What's Bliss and Bliss Land about? It's a place and we've given it a name but really it is about a feeling, a space and finding yourself. It's a space, a container, a safe haven for you to come and to find your own inner Bliss Land, to find your Heaven on Earth and to truly live in peace and joy whilst you are alive. So, my beautiful man, Lionel (my lion man), is creating this and bringing the vision to life.
My forte is Feng Shui, and his forte is Tantra. So together we are learning and connecting, joining the dots to create this beautiful map of Bliss Land. He has taught me about the beautiful connection between people, the real meaning and depth of a tantric connection. It's not just about sex

(the physical), it's about a deeper connection of mind, body and spirit, including also the connection between us all and being at one with nature and all that we truly are. Also, something I don't think I've ever mentioned to you before is that we have got twenty acres of land in Bliss Land, which is a huge amount of potential at our fingertips. Just recently within the last year, I met this amazing woman called Jean who created a programme called the Last Wishes Workshop and I invited her to Bliss Land to come and do one for us. My mum was ninety-one and came along to take part.
We all got to talk about dying - what we wanted when we died, where we wanted to be buried, and how. We didn't want our bodies to be embalmed because that toxic crap then goes straight back to the earth and pollutes the fresh, life-giving air. So many things that often don't get talked about or discussed and yet it's something that will inevitably happen to us all. It's a dead cert so to speak! I'm so very glad we did this workshop because what we could not have foreseen was that my mum actually died in March, and we buried her on International Happiness Day. So, it worked out just fine - perfectly in fact. I know that I fulfilled mum's wishes from having the knowledge and insights that I gained from that Last Wishes Workshop. Now I've gone on to set up a company with this lady and three other girls. We've called it' Live Your Legacy'. Teaching, encouraging and freeing people up in a safe and loving environment to be able to talk about death, which we are offering in these amazing Last Wishes Workshops.
So, for the last B - 'Burials'. We are going to bury people in Bliss Land. Statistically, about ninety-five per cent people are cremated, which is really environmentally unfriendly as we spoke about earlier - formaldehyde going into the air firstly, but also the energy consumption.
So, we want to teach people about this and offer better options; and let them know they have choices, and to be able to offer help and assistance in making the process of death as peaceful and beautiful as we can, to honour and

celebrate a life lived. So, the idea is to sell off plots of land where people can have a tree planted above them so that their bodies will then fertilise the trees and give back to the earth. Almost like a beautiful continuation of the circle of life. Planning permission is in, and we are hoping to start that in the next year.

Chery I believe you also offer other courses and workshops too, Dawn? Would you like to share a bit about them with us today?

Dawn Yes, we absolutely do. The courses we offer are designed to help you to be able to 'live happy' to really find your purpose, passion, and power. So, I will be teaching a lot about Feng Shui and then also a huge focus of ours is how to 'Love happy'. Lionel and I are working on a book which will be published in February next year and it's called 'Dare to Love'. In this book, there will be all sorts of techniques you can use to discover and really find that deep connection with your partner or loved one. Or, if you're still searching, tips, tools, and techniques on how to manifest and attract them into your life. So, it's all very exciting.

Cheryl And you've got another book that you're working on it as well, haven't you? You're a really busy lady!

Dawn Yes, I'm writing a book called 'Dare to Be Different' because people hear about me, they look at me and often want to know how I did it. How did I become a millionaire? How did I run that global business? How did I get thirty offices around the world? How did I find my soulmate?
Bang, bang, bang, bang, - questions all the time. So, I thought "what better way to answer all these questions than covering them all separately in the chapters of a book for people to read?" It means I get to share, and I love that.

Cheryl Another thing you're passionate about, Dawn, and something that brings you joy is your little grandchildren. I know you love to spend time with them, and you share a beautiful connection with them. I believe there is a bit of a thing around 'Storytime with Grandma?'

Dawn Oh yes, they bring so much joy to my heart and soul and there is so much laughter. Another idea we have, which I haven't shared with you until now, stemmed from a conversation with my daughter. She runs a vegan cafe called 'Wild and Wild' and she's asked me if I would come and be a storyteller there on occasion. So, of course, I jumped at the chance. I got all dressed up with a crazy hat and cape and I like to call my character 'The Wild Grandma', so I can't wait to do lots more of that. In the woods in Bliss Land, I think I'm going to be creating some little walkways called the 'Wild Bear Woods' where 'The Wild Grandma' will come and share her stories. Sitting around on logs with a campfire roaring.

So there are a lot of exciting things in the pipeline.

But yeah, what really makes me happy is my little squidgy grandchildren. I've got five of them - River, Jeffie, Grayson, Wild and little Ollie. They come and stay with me and we go on holiday together. I'm definitely the wild grandma who takes them out into the woods and gets them all mucky as I help and encourage them to connect with nature. It's magical.

Cheryl It kind of comes back to that whole concept of the circle of life because if you can teach them to love nature to begin with, and to feel grounded, alive and at home in their environment and excited to explore it, then this will really serve them. What a wonderful grandma to have. Dawn we could sit and talk for hours. I will have to invite you to come back again. But thank you for sharing how you live your life and what you love. We can really clearly see what you're passionate about and also what makes you laugh. Thank you so much for making a difference in the world, and for daring to be different and I very much look forward to seeing you next time. If you would like to find out more about Dawn Gibbons and the wonderful inspiring work the remarkable contribution she made to society, please take a look at her website: *www.blissland.co.uk*

Why Now?

Why now is the time to act, to begin your journey as a speaker... The last time I saw Dawn was in December 2021.

I was sitting in the Congleton Marks and Spencer's cafe, I looked to see her but was surprised that she was at the same level as me, strange as I was sitting on a chair. Then I saw her, half the weight and in a wheelchair. I resisted the urge to say 'How are you', it seemed so obvious that she wasn't that well. so instead I asked 'what's happening' 'Well Cheryl, they've told me I've got 6 weeks left to live - you know I wish I had written that book and been seen more, to help even more people'

In true Dawn fashion she defied the 6 weeks diagnosis, however, unfortunately she did pass after 8 weeks.

Knowing that Dawn with all her energy, wealth and happiness, still died with regret has been such a motivation for myself and others to STOP saying 'I'll think about it' and START saying I'm in, what would you say YES to today?

Little did we know that this would be the last presentation she would ever do.

See Dawn sharing her WHYs Words at the Live

Love Laugh Lives in October 2020 via this:
YouTube link: *https://youtu.be/LKW7A_Ewbnw*

"Dare To Be Different"

This book is dedicated to anyone who helped someone
else feels better, with a listening ear, a support
I've smile, a hug or some words of wisdom.

Thank you for being an Everyday Influencer

This book is also dedicated to those who stand up and speak their truth, from the heart, with an intention to share their wisdom, to educate, entertain and/or enlighten. Even if your words are not always heard or agreed with, thank you for sharing.

Thank you for being a speaker

This book is dedicated to those who trust themselves enough to be judged for what they believe and are passionate about.

Thank you for being a WHYs One

"Forgive them for they know not what they do".
Luke 23:34

About The Author

Cheryl Chapman is a multi-award-winning International Speaker and Mentor.

She has mentored thousands of speakers to share their messages in an authentic way, so that they can be seen, be heard and be themselves.

The award-winning co-author of Find Your WHY book and visionary at The Find Your WHY Foundation she guides women to find the clarity and the confidence to be the person they were born to be #frickinawesome

Cheryl is trained the following areas of coaching:

- Life Coaching
- NLP Master Practitioner
- Human Design - Level 4
- 64 Keys
- Genius Report
- Advanced RTT Therapist
- Clinical Hypnotherapist
- And 60 years around the sun

Creator of The Find Your Why Formula & The Confidently Come Speaking System.

WHYs Words

Who is Cheryl?

In Energy Terms a 959 Fire

Born in the year of The Dragon

In Human Design/Genetic Blueprint – A Projector/Architect

In Life an Action Taker, Straight-Talker, wife to Mr C and finally, she is Human (but don't let anyone know)

Available for speaking, mentoring, and guiding in groups or 1:1

Printed in Great Britain
by Amazon

43505176R00116